The Big Picture Family Devotional

The Big Picture

FAMILY DEVOTIONAL

edited by David R. Helm

CROSSWAY

WHEATON, ILLINOIS

The Big Picture Family Devotional

Copyright © 2014 by Holy Trinity Church

Published by Crossway
       1300 Crescent Street
       Wheaton, Illinois 60187

Cover Illustration: Gail Schoonmaker

First printing 2014

Printed in the United States of America

Scripture quotations are from the ESV® Bible (*The Holy Bible, English Standard Version®*), copyright © 2001 by Crossway. 2011 Text Edition. Used by permission. All rights reserved.

All emphases in Scripture quotations have been added by the author.

Trade paperback ISBN: 978-1-4335-4225-1
ePub ISBN: 978-1-4335-4228-2
PDF ISBN: 978-1-4335-4226-8
Mobipocket ISBN: 978-1-4335-4227-5

Library of Congress Cataloging-in-Publication Data

The big picture family devotional / David R. Helm.
    pages cm
   ISBN 978-1-4335-4225-1 (tp)
    1. Families—Religious life. 2. Christian education of children. 3. Christian education—Home training. 4. Families—Prayers and devotions. I. Helm, David R., 1961– editor.
BV4526.3.B54   2014
242'.2—dc23   2014005724

Crossway is a publishing ministry of Good News Publishers.

VP   24   23   22   21   20   19   18   17   16   15   14
15   14   13   12   11   10   9   8   7   6   5   4   3   2   1

Contents

Part 5
God Completes His Promise
Questions 37–45

Acknowledgments

One of the immense privileges of pastoring a church plant is the opportunity to colabor in the gospel with eager and energetic Christians—people who put their desire to make an impact for Christ to work by experimenting with new ideas to strengthen the church. In that context, *The Big Picture Family Devotional* was born.

In the fall of 1996, in the very early days of our church plant in Chicago, a commitment arose to provide fresh gospel resources for the many young families who were instructing their children in the faith. Because we believe the home is the central place for Christian education, the idea of writing a family devotional made sense. Soon afterward, the church was buzzing with excitement as members began writing devotional material that attempted to trace the storyline of the Bible. We even found ourselves writing Sunday school curriculum and adult small group study guides to supplement what was taking place around our dinner tables. Kids and adults alike began memorizing forty-five big picture verses that function as windows through which we gaze at God's unfolding promise. It was during these years that God also allowed me the privilege of writing *The Big Picture Story Bible*, beautifully illustrated by Gail Schoonmaker.

I would like to express my deep appreciation to Graeme Goldsworthy, whose ideas on biblical theology provided a springboard for us, as well as my admiration for the many members of Holy Trinity Church, Chicago, who joyfully labored in writing bits and pieces of what you now hold in your hands. *The Big Picture Family Devotional* is not the work of one person, but many—too many to mention them all by name! Special thanks go to Helen-Joy Lynerd for helping me prepare this book for publication. Also, I am indebited to Tara Davis of Crossway for her careful editing of the manuscript.

Finally, I want to acknowledge the children of Holy Trinity Church, Chicago—for you we gladly labor, counting it sweet joy.

How to Use This Devotional

The difficulty of devotions. Most people find doing family devotions difficult. For starters, many of us never had devotions modeled at home. Even if we were fortunate enough to grow up in a home with parents who tried to teach us the basics of religious belief, we must admit that today is a different world—one that presents us with practical challenges most of our parents never faced. Let's face it: today a family often eats meals at different times. Getting everyone together in the same place at the same time is nearly impossible.

How to use this devotional. Take heart! We live in the same world you do, and have written *The Big Picture Family Devotional* especially for today's family. Getting through this devotional in one year requires only three times a week when your family is in the same place at the same time. We even limited the material to fifty rather than fifty-two weeks so you can put this down and do something else for devotions during the weeks of Christmas and Easter. The devotional contains forty-five weeks of content and five weeks of review spread throughout the year. Everything is already prepared for you, saving you the time of trying to figure out something productive to share with your kids. Just open up the book and read the short Bible selection for the day and the brief devotional paragraph that unfolds the message of the Bible. Follow that up with the reflection and interaction prompts that are meant to spur family discussion. The entire process can take as little as five to ten minutes— or longer, at those unexpected but enjoyable leisurely times when your kids are particularly interested.

The devotional is geared for children ages six to ten, with the intention that it will be read through over several years so that the concepts are reinforced and children grow into an understanding of the more advanced ideas.

For those who want more. For families who like to sing, we have included songs that reinforce what you are learning together. For the highly motivated, we encourage you to make use of the forty-five memory verses that trace the big picture of the Bible. We call them the *big picture verses*, and a little booklet containing just the verses is available (titled *The Big Picture Verses: Tracing the Storyline of the Bible*). The verses can easily work as a catechism that takes you from Genesis to Revelation.

The word *catechism* comes from the Greek *katēchein*, which means "to teach." *The Big Picure Bible Verses* is a tool that will help parents teach their children the storyline of the Bible through questions and answers.

We hope *The Big Picture Devotional* will help clarify the main message of the Bible and instill in your family a growing confidence that the words of the Bible are the very words of God!

PART 1

God Creates His Kingdom

Questions 1–9

God Creates a Place

Q. Who created the heavens and the earth?

A. In the beginning, God created the heavens and the earth. (Genesis 1:1)

Bible Reading: Genesis 1:1

Devotional Reading: The Bible Assumes God's Existence

The Bible opens with these amazing words: "In the beginning, *God*." Have you ever stood outside at night and looked up into the stars and wondered, "How did all this get here? How did I get here?" In its very first verse, the Bible reveals the answer to those questions. The Bible says that God exists and that he created the heavens and the earth! Many people question whether God exists. Some are certain there is a God, others are unsure, while still others think that God is only an idea in your mind and not real after all. But guess what? The Bible doesn't waste any time arguing about the existence of God. It simply begins by saying, "In the beginning, *God*." How refreshing! The first words of the Bible are already hinting at its *big picture*—the unfolding activity of God in history.

REFLECTION AND INTERACTION

Memorize the question and answer of our first big picture verse: Genesis 1:1.

What does today's Bible reading teach you about God?

> Q. Who created the heavens and the earth?
>
> A. In the beginning, God created the heavens and the earth. (Genesis 1:1)

Bible Reading: Genesis 1:1–2

Devotional Reading: The Bible Begins with God Creating the Heavens and the Earth

Have you ever wanted to create something? Perhaps you had an idea in your head and you wondered if you could make it. Let's suppose you were going to try. What is one of the first things you would need to do before starting? You would have to gather all the materials your idea needed. Did you know that God did something like that when he created the world? When God set out to create the heavens and the earth he first had to create the materials themselves! The Bible tells us that when God first made the earth, it was only a dark and watery mass. The basic materials were all there, but it didn't look the way it does now. It looked strange. Nothing could live on it—certainly not people like you and me! How amazing it would have been to see God creating and assembling all the materials he needed to make his wonderful creation.

REFLECTION AND INTERACTION

Would you say the Bible reading today is more concerned to teach you about the *heavens* or the *earth*?

What does the Bible's concern with the earth here tell you about the focus of Genesis 1?

Q. **Who created the heavens and the earth?**

A. In the beginning, God created the heavens and the earth. (Genesis 1:1)

Bible Reading: Genesis 1:3–25

Devotional Reading: God Formed Places and Then Filled Them

Often when you want to color a picture of something, you first draw, or form, the outline of the object or person to be colored and then fill in the color. Well, something like that is going on in Genesis 1. It's as if the writer gives us an outline of what happened in the first few verses and then fills in the details later in the chapter. The creation outline of day 1 gets filled in on day 4. On day 1 we learn about light and darkness, day and night. Then on day 4, we are introduced to the sun and the moon and the stars, which fill up the sky. Isn't that amazing! The outline of day 2 (the heavens and the seas) is filled in on day 5 (the birds and sea creatures). And day 3 (the earth and plants) corresponds to day 6 (the land animals). The writer wants you to see the overall picture of God's creative activity. He wants you to know that God *formed* all the places in the universe (days 1, 2, and 3), and then *filled* those places with creations to rule over them (days 4, 5, and 6). Finally, notice that the writer says God did all this simply by speaking words (see vv. 3, 6, 9, 11, 14–15, 20, and 24)! Imagine creating something that was an idea in your head by talking it into existence!

REFLECTION AND INTERACTION

Can you create things simply by speaking words? What does God's ability to do so teach you about God?

Learn "The Creation Song" found on pages 174–75.

God Creates a People

> **Q. Who created people?**
>
> **A.** God created man in his own image, in the image of God he created him; male and female he created them. (Genesis 1:27)

Bible Reading: Genesis 1:26–31

Devotional Reading: People Are Created in God's Image

The Bible makes it clear that people are very special to God. In fact, we are the crowning jewel of God's creation. God did not make people to be like the rest of creation, "God created man *in His own image, in the image of God* he created him; male and female he created them." An image is a reflection of someone or something. When you look in the mirror, you see your own reflection, or image. God made us to reflect *his* image. That doesn't mean we look like God. Instead, it means that we are like him; we rule over things, just as God does. In ancient times, kings used to set up monuments in faraway parts of their empire to show that they ruled there (often these monuments were statues made to look just like them). In a similar way, God has set us up to rule over his creation. As his image-bearers, we act as his representatives in the world. Later on in the Bible story, the psalmist will pick up on this same idea (Psalm 8), and then, the writer of the book of Hebrews will show us that Jesus is God's supreme image-bearer (Heb. 2:5–8). This is important for us because it teaches us how we extend God's rule today—namely, by living under the rule of Christ.

REFLECTION AND INTERACTION

What does being made in the image of God teach you about God's plans for you?

Memorize the big picture verse for this week: Genesis 1:27. If you memorize one each week, you will learn all forty-five verses that trace the storyline of the Bible!

Q. Who created people?

A. God created man in his own image, in the image of God he created him; male and female he created them. (Genesis 1:27)

Bible Reading: Genesis 2:18–25

Devotional Reading: People Are the Pinnacle of God's Creation

Have you ever seen a road map? It's helpful because it shows you many roads. Some maps even come with an inset map. This highlights in greater detail one part of the road map. Genesis 1 and 2 function much like a road map. After giving us the large map of creation in chapter 1, God highlights the most important part of creation in chapter 2—people! He wants you to see the creation of people in greater detail. The point is clear: God created this place for people. We learn that Adam loved everything about his life in the garden, except for one thing: he was alone. The animals all had partners, but not Adam. In fact, one of the reasons God had Adam name the animals was to prepare him for Eve. God said, "It is not good that man should be alone; I will make him a helper." So God had Adam fall into a deep sleep. While Adam was sleeping, God took one of Adam's ribs, and from this rib he "built" a woman. As only God could do, he created the perfect companion for Adam. This teaches us another thing about being made in God's image. We are meant for relationship. Not only does man have a special relationship with woman, but both men and women have a unique relationship with God.

REFLECTION AND INTERACTION

Why did God ask Adam to name all the animals?

What was special about Adam's relationship with Eve that was different from his relationship with God's other creatures?

Q. Who created people?

A. God created man in his own image, in the image of God he created him; male and female he created them. (Genesis 1:27)

Bible Reading: Genesis 1:26–31

Devotional Reading: People Are to Rule over the Rest of God's Creation

When children are born, who is responsible for them? Parents are. Parents prepare meals, teach their children to get dressed, and help them learn what is right from wrong. Parents are responsible for their children. Do you know who is responsible for caring for God's creation? All of us are. When God created the world and everything in it, he made us responsible for his creation. God gave us the wonderful responsibility of ruling over and caring for all that he created. That means the entire earth and everything in it. It is God's world, but he appointed us to rule it for him.

REFLECTION AND INTERACTION

Discuss some ways that we care for God's world.

Can you think of some ways that we rule God's world?

God Is Pleased with His Place and His People

> **Q. Was God pleased with everything he had made?**
>
> A. God saw everything that he had made, and behold, it was very good. (Genesis 1:31)

Bible Reading: Genesis 1:3–4, 10, 12, 16–18, 21, 25, 31

Devotional Reading: God's Creation Was Very Good

Let's try to remember some things about God's creation. How did creation get started? God said, "Let there be light," and there was light. God separated the light from the darkness, day and night. Water and sky are listed next, followed by dry ground, which he called land, and the great bodies of water, which he called seas. God caused plants and trees to grow on the land, and then the sun, the moon, and all the stars. Next were fish in the seas, birds in the sky, and animals to live on the land. Finally God created people. Can you remember what God thought about each and everything that he created? The Bible tells us "it was very good." It was just as God had planned it. He was happy with his place and with his people. Nothing was wrong. Everything was just as he had envisioned it in his mind before he began. Everything was good!

REFLECTION AND INTERACTION

Does everything you make turn out just as you planned it? What does the goodness of God's creation teach you about God?

This is a great week to sing "It Was Very Good" found on page 176.

Begin to memorize this week's big picture verse: Genesis 1:31.

> Q. **Was God pleased with everything he had made?**
>
> A. God saw everything that he had made, and behold, it was very good. (Genesis 1:31)

Bible Reading: Psalm 104:24–31

Devotional Reading: God's Place and People Gave Him Great Pleasure

What does it feel like to make something very special? It feels good, doesn't it? You feel proud. Making something gives you a certain amount of pleasure and satisfaction. It makes you happy. Imagine how pleased God was after making the world and everything in it! The Bible reading today teaches us that God was extremely happy with all that he had created. We read, "May the glory of the LORD endure [or *last*] forever; *may the LORD rejoice in his works*." The Lord was pleased with all he had created, and he rejoiced in it. The place and people were made *for* God!

REFLECTION AND INTERACTION

Why do you think God created this beautiful place called *earth* and all of its people?

Name some things in the world that you think still give God great pleasure.

> **Q. Was God pleased with everything he had made?**
>
> A. God saw everything that he had made, and behold, it was very good. (Genesis 1:31)

Bible Reading: Colossians 1:15–20

Devotional Reading: The Eternal Son of God Had a Role in Creation

What are some good things about having an older brother or sister? One advantage of not being born first is that you can learn some things faster by watching your older sibling. The Bible demonstrates the same principle. Our New Testament writer today had an advantage in coming later. He learned some interesting things from others who had gone before him—in this case, that the world was created by the eternal Son of God, who was later born into the world and named Jesus. Jesus is the *big picture* in God's story, the Bible. Before we leave the first chapter of the Bible, we must understand that the eternal Son of God had a lot to do with what happened in the beginning. He was involved in creating everything and is in charge of everything. Perhaps what is most astounding is that he created all things for himself. Since this eternal Son of God is our Creator and King, and since he alone sustains this beautiful place and all its people, he alone deserves all our praise.

REFLECTION AND INTERACTION

Why should we worship the Son of God?

How does it make you feel to know that all creation was made for Jesus?

God Is King over His Place and His People

> **Q. What command did God give his people to obey?**
>
> A. [From] the tree of the knowledge of good and evil you shall not eat, for in the day that you eat of it you shall surely die. (Genesis 2:17)

Bible Reading: Genesis 2:15–17

Devotional Reading: God Rules His People by His Word

Do you like being told what you can and cannot do? Why not? After giving Adam and Eve the most beautiful garden ever, the first thing God did was tell them what they could and could not do. He gave them a simple command. Out of all the trees in the garden, there was one from which they could not eat. If they ate from it, they would die. In this command God makes it clear to us that he is a King who rules over Adam and Eve. God has authority over them, just as a king has authority over his kingdom. And just as children should obey parents, Adam and Eve were to obey God. If they did not, they would be punished. Too often people think they can do whatever they like. However, the Bible teaches us that people are meant to live under God's Word.

REFLECTION AND INTERACTION

Did God make us in such a way that we can live life in whatever way we choose?

What does God's command to Adam and Eve teach you about the relationship between God and people?

Memorize this week's big picture verse: Genesis 2:17.

> **Q. What command did God give his people to obey?**
>
> A. [From] the tree of the knowledge of good and evil you shall not eat, for in the day that you eat of it you shall surely die. (Genesis 2:17)

Bible Reading: Genesis 1:29–31

Devotional Reading: Life Is Good under God's Word

The garden of Eden was the most beautiful place in the world. The trees stood tall and cast cool shade over the soft green grass. Birds sang beautiful songs. No one suffered from deadly diseases, and people didn't die. This was the "good life" for Adam and Eve in the garden of Eden. They didn't have to struggle in their work, because God provided everything they needed. When the Bible says that life in the garden was good, it means good for the purpose for which God created it. Everything was very nice. By obeying God, Adam and Eve would continue to enjoy God and his magnificent garden. Imagine how great life must have been when everything was "very good" under God's word.

REFLECTION AND INTERACTION

Do you think that you would have enjoyed living under God's word?

What do you think would have been the best part of life in the garden?

> **Q. What command did God give his people to obey?**
>
> A. [From] the tree of the knowledge of good and evil you shall not eat, for in the day that you eat of it you shall surely die. (Genesis 2:17)

Bible Reading: Genesis 2:16–17; Ephesians 2:1–3

Devotional Reading: What God Means by "You Shall Surely Die"

In our first reading today, God tells Adam and Eve that they will die if they disobey his word. God is teaching them that to have life, they need to obey. If they disobey, not only will their physical bodies die, but they will also have a spiritual death. Here's an illustration that might help you understand how that works. Once upon a time there was a kite. This kite loved to fly high overhead in the big blue sky. In fact, this kite wanted to go higher and higher and higher, but eventually, the length of the string held it back. It couldn't fly any higher. Then the kite thought, "What if I break away from this string? Then I could go as high as I wanted." What would really happen if the kite broke away from the string? Would it fly higher than ever? No, it would plummet to the ground and break into pieces. The string that holds the kite back also provides the resistance that allows it to fly in the first place. If you or I—like Adam and Eve—were to cut loose from God's word, we would find out that we need God's word to live in the first place. Without God's word, we would return to the earth from which we were created and die, both physically and spiritually.

REFLECTION AND INTERACTION

What does the punishment of death tell you about God's character?

How seriously does God take your obedience to his word?

God's People Reject God as King

Q. Did God's people obey God's word?

A. [Eve] took of its fruit and ate, and she also gave some to her husband who was with her, and he ate. (Genesis 3:6)

Bible Reading: Genesis 3:6–13

Devotional Reading: Adam and Eve's Sin Was Rejecting God as King

Despite all God's goodness to Adam and Eve, our Bible reading today makes it clear that they chose to disobey his command—they cut themselves loose from God's word. They rebelled against God as King. They did not, and would not, live under his word. Eve allowed Satan's voice to convince her that eating the fruit would make her wise, so she ate it. Adam also, without any hesitation, joined Eve in disobeying God. Together they doubted God's goodness toward them. They thought that they could do a better job of being God. How horrible it is that they chose to rebel against their loving King! Their decision to disobey God was a sad event in the Bible because it brought about the first sin.

REFLECTION AND INTERACTION

Why do you think Adam and Eve chose to sin against God?

What is sin? Do you think any of us can completely stop from sinning?

Begin to memorize this week's big picture verse: Genesis 3:6.

> Q. **Did God's people obey God's word?**
>
> A. [Eve] took of its fruit and ate, and she also gave some to her husband who was with her, and he ate. (Genesis 3:6)

Bible Reading: Genesis 3:1–6

Devotional Reading: Adam and Eve's Temptation Was to Reject God's Goodness

Sometimes we show our love for people by giving them presents. God loved Adam and Eve so much that he gave them a gorgeous garden. The garden was to be their place, they were to be his people, and God was to be their God. By doing all of this for them, God was demonstrating to them that he was a good God. God did everything to protect them. But then Satan came into the garden in the form of a Serpent and convinced Adam and Eve that God was *not* good, despite all the wonderful things God had done. Satan convinced them that God was really trying to harm them by making rules and having special commands. Satan got them to believe that God was not caring, that he was not looking out for their good. And do you know what? Any time you are tempted, Satan uses the same trick. He tries to get you to doubt God's goodness.

REFLECTION AND INTERACTION

How has God shown you that he cares for you? Is it ever hard to believe that God loves you?

How do we know that God is good and doing what is best for us?

> **Q. Did God's people obey God's word?**
>
> **A.** [Eve] took of its fruit and ate, and she also gave some to her husband who was with her, and he ate. (Genesis 3:6)

Bible Reading: Genesis 3:1–6

Devotional Reading: Adam and Eve's Temptation
Was to Rebel against God's Word

God had given Adam and Eve one command. However, after Satan tempted Eve, she disobeyed God's command. Eve decided to rebel against the word of God and live under the voice of Satan. Eve was tempted to distrust God's word because she began to doubt God's goodness toward her. "After all," she may have thought to herself, "why can't Adam and I eat that fruit that looks so good? Perhaps God isn't as kind as I had first thought." So in the garden on that day, Eve (along with Adam, whom our text says was right there with her) failed to obey God. Adam and Eve trusted Satan's words more than God's. We can be tempted in the same way, when we begin to doubt God's goodness to us. If we doubt God's goodness, we may think that we can disobey God's word and do what seems more interesting or fun to us.

REFLECTION AND INTERACTION

When is it hard for you to do what God says? Why is it hard?

Name some different ways that Satan tempts you. What do those ways have to do with the goodness of God in your life?

God's Place Is Forever Changed

> **Q. How did God judge the Serpent?**
>
> A. I will put enmity between you and the woman, and between your offspring and her offspring; he shall bruise your head, and you shall bruise his heel. (Genesis 3:15)

Bible Reading: Genesis 2:8–9; 3:17–18

Devotional Reading: God's Place Is Now under His Curse

Have you ever tried to plant a tree, or flowers, or maybe even vegetables? It can be very hard to make them grow, can't it? You have to water them often, protect them from the cold, keep away bugs that want to eat them, and discourage squirrels who would come and dig them up. Remember that before Adam and Eve sinned, God had blessed them by planting a beautiful garden for them to live in. There God planted trees and plants and caused them to grow by watering and protecting them. Everything Adam and Eve needed, God gave to them. However, after they sinned, God did not make the trees and plants grow in the same way as before. God took his blessing away and he cursed the ground. Now we too have to protect ourselves from the wind, snow, and rain and even things like earthquakes and tornados. The world isn't a safe place anymore because God took away his blessing and cursed the ground. When Adam and Eve sinned, I don't think they could have possibly imagined the consequences it would have even up to today.

REFLECTION AND INTERACTION

What do you think the blessing of God means?

How did God curse the ground? What does that teach you about God's character?

Memorize this week's big picture verse: Genesis 3:15.

> **Q. How did God judge the Serpent?**
>
> A. I will put enmity between you and the woman, and between your offspring and her offspring; he shall bruise your head, and you shall bruise his heel. (Genesis 3:15)

Bible Reading: Genesis 3:14–15

Devotional Reading: God Judges the Serpent

Do you find some animals to be scary? Why are you afraid of them? The Bible describes Satan as different kinds of dangerous animals. Sometimes it calls him a roaring lion; other times a great red dragon. Today we learned that he is also called a lying Serpent. Satan lied to Eve through the Serpent because Satan is God's enemy and the enemy of all God's people. Because of what happened between Eve and the Serpent, God cursed the Serpent by making him crawl on the ground. God also judged Satan. In these verses, we learn through this verse that God will triumph over Satan in the end.

REFLECTION AND INTERACTION

What does God's ability to judge Satan teach you about God?

What are some ways you can protect yourself from our enemy Satan?

> **Q. How did God judge the Serpent?**
>
> A. I will put enmity between you and the woman, and between your offspring and her offspring; he shall bruise your head, and you shall bruise his heel. (Genesis 3:15)

Bible Reading: Genesis 3:15; Revelation 12:1–17

Devotional Reading: God Makes His First Promise of Grace

Close your eyes and try to picture an enormous red dragon. He has ten heads and ten horns on each head and a long tail that he swings back and forth, and he is very angry. Open your eyes. That big red dragon is one way the Bible describes Satan. What would you do to fight against a terrible red dragon? Do you know what God was planning to do? Our memory verse this week teaches us that God chose to defeat the dragon with a child who is a descendant of Eve! Do you know who that child is? The book of Revelation says that Jesus is the baby who was promised to Adam and Eve in the garden. He is the One born to crush and defeat Satan. Isn't it great to learn that even at this most tragic point in the Bible, God promises to rescue Adam and Eve from their own sin through one of Eve's distant children? God's promise of rescue goes all the way back to the garden of Eden. The rest of the Old Testament shows us how and when God would bring Jesus into the world to defeat Satan.

REFLECTION AND INTERACTION

What does God promise to do in Genesis 3:15?

Take time to pray and thank God for sending Jesus to defeat Satan.

God's People Are Forced Out

Q. How did the Lord God judge his people?

A. The LORD God sent [them] out from the garden of Eden. (Genesis 3:23)

Bible Reading: Genesis 3:16–24

Devotional Reading: God's People Can No Longer Live in God's Place

What is the worst punishment you can think of? In our Bible reading today, God brings about several punishments because of Adam and Eve's sin. While God still allows Eve the gift of having children, childbirth will now be very painful. While God still maintains the gift of marriage, the relationship between the husband and the wife will now be difficult. While God continues the gift of work, it will now be very, very hard. And while God allows Adam and Eve to continue to live, one day they will surely die. But the worst punishment of all is when God forces Adam and Eve to leave the garden of Eden. God's people are forced out of the place God made for them. This was terrible because the garden of Eden was where God's presence was. Since Adam and Eve no longer have the special relationship they once enjoyed with God, they can no longer live in his presence. God had to throw them out of the garden and away from his presence.

REFLECTION AND INTERACTION

Even though Adam and Eve sinned against God, God still blessed them in many ways. What does that tell you about God?

Try memorizing the big picture verse for this week: Genesis 3:23. Review some past ones too.

> Q. How did the Lord God judge his people?
>
> A. The LORD God sent [them] out from the garden of Eden. (Genesis 3:23)

Bible Reading: Psalm 90:9–11

Devotional Reading: The World outside the Garden Is Very Difficult

The results of sin are all around us. When we go to the zoo, we have to look at the animals behind glass or tall fences or in cages, because when sin entered the world, our relationship with the animals changed. We get into fights with people and lie and take things that are not ours because of sin. When God created the world, he put everything in perfect order. There was peace between everyone. There was peace between God and Adam, there was peace between Adam and Eve, and there was peace between Adam and Eve and all the animals. However, outside the garden, all of these peaceful relationships were broken. Sin is why we now live in a world where God is angry with people, people hurt one another, and we no longer live in relationship to God or rule his world as we were supposed to.

REFLECTION AND INTERACTION

Does the Bible give us a reason why the world is in the sad state that it is in?

What are you learning about the effects of Adam and Eve's sin?

Q. How did the Lord God judge his people?

A. The LORD God sent [them] out from the garden of Eden. (Genesis 3:23)

Bible Reading: Romans 5:12–21

Devotional Reading: We Are All Sinners
Who Need God to Rescue Us

Have you ever noticed that many children look a lot like their parents? Parents pass down traits to their children—traits like looks, abilities, and personality. We are all children of Adam and Eve, and we are like them in important ways. When they sinned and disobeyed God's word, they became sinners. Because Adam and Eve are the first parents, and everyone living today is descended from them, we are like them; we are sinners too. Because we are sinners, we are under the same curses as Adam and Eve. The greatest curse we are under is the curse of death. When the Bible speaks of death, it means more than just growing old and having our bodies die. Death is also a broken relationship with God—living apart from him forever. The worst part about this is that we can do nothing to change it. That is why we need God to rescue us. God's rescue is what the Bible is all about. The big picture of the Bible is how he rescues us from our own sin.

REFLECTION AND INTERACTION

Do you normally think of yourself as a sinner or as a good person?

What is the Bible teaching you about how God sees you?

Take time to review all of the big picture verses you have been learning.

Everyone Now Rejects God as King

> Q. **What did God see on the earth?**
>
> A. God saw the earth, and behold, it was corrupt, for all flesh had corrupted their way on the earth. (Genesis 6:12)

Bible Reading: Genesis 6:1–12

Devotional Reading: All of Adam and Eve's Offspring Rebel against God's Rule

Take a guess at what the word *corruption* means. You could think of it as bread that has gone moldy or as leaders who use their power to get something they want, no matter how it hurts other people. The Bible teaches us that after God removed Adam and Eve from the garden of Eden, all people became corrupt. Adam and Eve's children and their children after them were very wicked. All people sinned against God, just like their first parents. They did all sorts of evil things that God hated. Everyone did such bad things that God became sorry he had ever made people. Isn't it sad to see how far God's people had fallen from when God first made them? God had made the world as a place for his people, but his people refused to live under his word. The Bible teaches us that every single thing they thought about was corrupted with sin.

REFLECTION AND INTERACTION

The Bible says that God was sad that he had ever made people. What does that tell you about God's character?

Begin memorizing the big picture verse for the week: Genesis 6:12. (In two weeks' time, you will get a whole week to review the first nine verses!)

> **Q. What did God see on the earth?**
>
> A. God saw the earth, and behold, it was corrupt, for all flesh had corrupted their way on the earth. (Genesis 6:12)

Bible Reading: Romans 1:18–25

Devotional Reading: People Serve Creatures Rather Than the Creator

How would you feel if you worked your hardest on a beautiful finger painting only to discover that after you were done, everyone loved the painting but ignored you? Did you know that something like that happened to God? When God created the world, it became like his own painting. And his fingerprints are still everywhere to be seen (Psalm 8:3). Sadly though, very few people pay attention to God. We are too busy ignoring him and doing what we want with his painting. Think about the world for a moment. Remember, this is God's world. He made it. Do we act as if it is ours? Do we ignore God, who should be the central focus of our lives? Isn't it silly for us to choose to worship the things that God created rather than the God who created them? Don't forget: God is the master painter, and when we ignore him in favor of his creation, we are rejecting him as King.

REFLECTION AND INTERACTION

How do we act like the world is ours and not God's? Why do you think we do that?

What does our Bible reading say that God does about our rejecting him as King?

> **Q. What did God see on the earth?**
>
> A. God saw the earth, and behold, it was corrupt, for all flesh had corrupted their way on the earth. (Genesis 6:12)

Bible Reading: Romans 3:9–20

Devotional Reading: We All Are Sinners Who Deserve God's Wrath

Have you ever said things you shouldn't have, or gone places you were supposed to stay away from, or looked at things you should have avoided? The Bible reading for today teaches us that our tongues, our feet, and our eyes all do what is wrong. With our lips we all have lied. With our feet we have gone places we should not have gone. And with our eyes we have looked on things that were better left unseen. Our hearts are full of corruption and sin. We deserve to be punished by God. Some people find it hard to believe that everyone in the world is a sinner deserving of God's punishment. But the Bible says it's true. You and I are sinners. There's no way around it. We are all guilty of sin because we all come from Adam the sinner. We all deserve to be punished by God.

REFLECTION AND INTERACTION

What are you learning this week about the effects Adam and Eve's sin had on all of their children and children's children?

What are some of the things you think and do that tell you your heart is corrupt?

God Judges Everyone Who Rejects Him as King

Q. How did God promise to judge everything on the earth?

A. I will bring a flood of waters upon the earth to destroy all flesh. (Genesis 6:17)

Bible Reading: Genesis 6:5–8, 12–17

Devotional Reading: The Sadness and Anger of God

Do you remember what God said shortly after he created the earth? He called his entire creation good—*very* good! It gave him great pleasure. However, when Adam and Eve disobeyed God, God's heart was filled with pain. The people he created to live in this place, the very people who were created for a special loving relationship with him, were now rejecting him all the time. There was only one man who tried to love God and live by his word—Noah. God told Noah how sorry he was that he had made men and women. He told Noah that he was going to punish everyone who rejected him as King by sending a great flood. God told Noah to build a big boat, an ark, to save himself and his family from the flood that was about to come.

REFLECTION AND INTERACTION

Why was God happy with Noah and not happy with all the other people who lived at that time?

This is the perfect week to sing "The Flood Song" found on page 177.

Begin to memorize this week's big picture verse: Genesis 6:17.

> Q. **How did God promise to judge everything on the earth?**
>
> A. I will bring a flood of waters upon the earth to destroy all flesh. (Genesis 6:17)

Bible Reading: Genesis 7:6–24

Devotional Reading: God's Holiness Demanded the Flood

God is holy. Do you know what it means for God to be *holy*? In part, it means that God is pure and perfect. He is entirely good. It means his thoughts and actions are always right and never evil. That makes God very different from people, doesn't it? God's holiness is what now separates him from the people he created. His holiness demands that those who reject him must be punished. Noah was six hundred years old when God told him to take his family and every kind of animal into the ark. God closed the door on the ark as it began to rain. It rained for forty days and forty nights, and the waters flooded the earth for one hundred and fifty days. Everyone perished, except Noah, his family, and the animals inside the ark. God's holiness demands that he punish sin and rescue the righteous, as he did for Noah.

REFLECTION AND INTERACTION

Do you think God unfairly punished people in Noah's day? Why or why not?

How would you define *holiness*?

> **Q. How did God promise to judge everything on the earth?**
>
> A. I will bring a flood of waters upon the earth to destroy all flesh. (Genesis 6:17)

Bible Reading: 2 Peter 3:3–10

Devotional Reading: God's Hatred of Sin Requires a Final Judgment

When someone makes a dress, she often works from a pattern. The pattern isn't to be confused with the real dress, which will come later. A pattern helps us to see what the real dress will look like. The Bible is filled with patterns, and the flood is one of them. The flood points us to the real and final judgment of God that is yet to come. When the final judgment comes, God will not destroy the world by water, but by fire. Many people don't believe God will ever judge anyone. They think that because God is loving, he will overlook everyone's sin. But that is just not true. God never overlooks sin; he cannot. The Bible reading today teaches us that the pattern for God's final judgment is seen in the flood. The rest of the Bible unfolds God's plan to rescue people from his judgment through the one man who is righteous.

REFLECTION AND INTERACTION

Knowing that the flood sets the pattern for the fact that God will judge the world again, what might you change about how you think and act?

Take a minute to thank God for the Bible, which tells you of his plan to rescue you from his judgment.

God Creates His Kingdom

Review 1: Reviewing the Memory Verses

One way we can help our children learn is to begin memorizing portions of God's Word with them. The beauty of these catechism questions is just that. They are selected verses from the Bible! *The Big Picture Family Devotional* is not systematic theology—it doesn't ask you to learn about God through the categories of human invention. Rather it is about biblical theology—you learn the Bible as it was given to us by God in the first place. If you and your children will commit to memorizing all the big picture verses in this devotional, you will have helped them and yourself be able to trace the storyline of the Bible. Take time this week to plant God's Word in your heart.

Review the big picture verses for the past nine weeks.

Review 2: Reviewing the Plotline of Genesis 1–11

It is important for you and your children to grasp the overall flow of the first nine weeks. One way to do this is to reread the titles over each week's question and answer. You could say something like, "Let me see if I can summarize all that we have been learning about. We saw that God Creates a Place ➤ God Creates a People ➤ God Is Pleased with His Place and His People ➤ God Is King over His Place and His People ➤ God's People Reject God as King ➤ God's Place Is Forever Changed ➤ God's People Are Forced Out ➤ Everyone Now Rejects God as King ➤ God Judges Everyone Who Rejects Him as King."

Spend some time today reinforcing the big picture of these past nine weeks.

Review 3: Learning by an Ancient and Big Word Called the *Trivium*

We all need certain things to be able to learn. The *trivium* is a big-sounding way of stating the three things we need in order for true learning to take place. First is *grammar*. Grammar provides the building blocks for learning. Second, we need *logic*. We must be able to see the relationships between the itty-bitty parts of grammar. For instance, we learn the relationship between numbers like 2 and 22 and 222. Logic is the process of understanding how things coherently flow together. Third, we need *rhetoric*. Rhetoric tests our ability to communicate what we know. It is the tough part of restating things in such a way as to show we truly get it.

The Big Picture Family Devotional gives you a chance to work on all three areas with your children. The grammar is the memory verses. Logic is understanding how each verse relates to the others to create a coherent plotline or story. And the review weeks are the time for rhetoric. They allow you to test yourselves in your ability to restate what these nine weeks have been about. Be encouraged. You are teaching your children how to think by using this devotional!

Keep working this week on memorizing the big picture verses and articulating the storyline.

PART 2

God Begins His Promise

Questions 10–18

God Promises a New Place to a New People, Who Will Bless All People

> **Q. How did the Lord begin his promise to rescue all peoples on earth?**
>
> A. The LORD said to Abra[ham], "Go . . . to the land that I will show you. And I will make of you a great nation, and I will bless you . . . and in you all the families of the earth shall be blessed." (Genesis 12:1–3)

Bible Reading: Genesis 12:1–5

Devotional Reading: God Takes the First Steps

Have you ever had to move? Perhaps you've moved to another house or apartment. Or maybe you know someone who has moved to another city or state. Moving can be exciting. It can also be difficult: lots of packing, lots of new things to learn, and a whole lot of new people to meet. In our Bible reading today, God told Abraham (Abraham is the name God gives him a little later on) to move his family to a faraway country. The hard part was that God didn't tell him exactly where to go. God just said, "Get going, and I'll show you where." You see, God was taking steps to rescue all peoples from sin by choosing to work through this one person. Our big picture verse this week shows just how much God cares about us. Abraham obeyed God's command. He was seventy-five years old when he and his family left Haran and faithfully followed God's word. When you think of Abraham, remember that through him God was announcing his plan to rescue us from sin.

REFLECTION AND INTERACTION

What does God's promise to Abraham teach you about God?

Do you think it was easy for Abraham to follow God's leading? Why or why not?

Memorize this week's big picture verse: Genesis 12:1–3.

> Q. **How did the Lord begin his promise to rescue all peoples on earth?**
>
> A. The LORD said to Abra[ham], "Go . . . to the land that I will show you. And I will make of you a great nation, and I will bless you . . . and in you all the families of the earth shall be blessed." (Genesis 12:1–3)

Bible Reading: Genesis 12:1–5

Devotional Reading: God Promises to Bless All Peoples

Do you like it when someone does something nice for you? God's promise of blessing wasn't just for Abraham; God was doing something special for people from every people group who would believe his promise. And that includes you and me! God promised to make Abraham the leader of a great nation that would live in a special place. God promised that Abraham's name would be great, and then, through Abraham, God's blessing would spread to all peoples on the earth. God chose Abraham to start the big picture plan to rescue all peoples from sin and judgment. Through Abraham, everyone who believes will be blessed. What a great and wonderful promise! God is going to establish a new *people*, have them live in a new *place*, and, under the power of his word, bless all *peoples* through it. When God made his big promise to Abraham, God was doing something nice for *you*.

REFLECTION AND INTERACTION

In earlier lessons we learned that all people sin against God. What do you learn about God through his promise to rescue people, even those who sin against him?

Do you see how God is going to restore a *people* and a *place*, and reverse the universal judgment we are all under through Adam and Eve's fall?

Q. How did the Lord begin his promise to rescue all peoples on earth?

A. The LORD said to Abra[ham], "Go . . . to the land that I will show you. And I will make of you a great nation, and I will bless you . . . and in you all the families of the earth shall be blessed." (Genesis 12:1-3)

Bible Reading: Genesis 12:1–3; 15:1–5

Devotional Reading: God's Story Has Big Plans for Many People

Have you ever tried to count the twinkling stars in a dark night sky? It's hard work because there are so many of them. God told Abraham to go outside and try to count every star he could see. As Abraham started counting, God promised him that the blessing he was giving him would extend to his children, and his children's children, and his children's children's children. God said that it would include so many people that to count them all would be like trying to count the stars in the sky. Do you know why this is such an amazing promise? At the time God made it, Abraham didn't have any children at all—not even one! That ought to tell us something about the power of God. He was promising an old man who had no children that he would one day be the father of many peoples.

REFLECTION AND INTERACTION

What does God's promise to Abraham teach you about his love for the world?

What does such a promise from God teach you about his desire to get all the glory for rescuing us from sin?

Abraham Believes God's Promise

Q. How did Abraham respond to the Lord's word?

A. [Abraham] believed the LORD, and he counted it to him as righteousness. (Genesis 15:6)

Bible Reading: Genesis 15:1–6

Devotional Reading: Abraham Believes

Put your thinking cap on—what do you know about the man named Abraham? Among other things, Abraham was the one person God chose to start his big rescue plan. He told him that not only would nations come from him, but kings too (see Genesis 17:1–6)! The only problem was that Abraham didn't have any children. How could a man have lots of descendants, even a royal line, if he didn't even have a single child? Abraham couldn't possibly know how this could happen, but God told him it would. And do you know what? Abraham believed the Lord. He trusted that what God said was true. He believed that God was good, and not a liar. Abraham's faith pleased God. God will be very pleased with you too if you trust that his words are true. Faith is trusting and believing that God's word is true. Faith is believing in God's word even when it doesn't seem to make sense, even when you're not sure of what's ahead. The Bible tells us in Hebrews 11:6 that "without faith it is impossible to please [God]."

REFLECTION AND INTERACTION

How would you describe faith to someone else?

This is a great week to sing "I Will Have Faith in God" found on page 180.

Begin to memorize this week's big picture verse: Genesis 15:6.

> **Q. How did Abraham respond to the Lord's word?**
>
> A. [Abraham] believed the LORD, and he counted it to him as righteousness. (Genesis 15:6)

Bible Reading: Romans 4:1–8

Devotional Reading: Abraham's Faith Was Not from Good Works

What is it that God wants from us? Abraham did a lot of good things in his life. However, the Bible says that God only considered him righteous—that is, declared free from guilt—because of his faith (even his faith was a gift from God, according to Ephesians 2:8–9)! Many people today think that all God wants is for us to do good works. They forget that we are *all* sinners. Even Abraham wasn't perfect. Like you and me, he broke God's laws at times. He said, thought, and did things that displeased God. The only way God could call Abraham righteous was by giving him righteousness as a gift. Good works weren't enough then, and they aren't enough now. The Bible reading today tells us that no one can come to know God by trying harder. We all need faith. Faith is what God wants, and demands, of us.

REFLECTION AND INTERACTION

List some good things you've done during this week. According to the Bible, are they enough to make you righteous in the sight of a holy and perfect God?

If you can't ever fully obey God because of sin, then how can you become righteous?

> **Q. How did Abraham respond to the Lord's word?**
>
> **A.** [Abraham] believed the LORD, and he counted it to him as righteousness. (Genesis 15:6)

Bible Reading: Galatians 3:1–9

Devotional Reading: People Will Be Rescued by Faith

Have you ever wondered how anyone gets into heaven? Try to think of what you must do to win God's favor. Many people believe that to get into heaven, they have to do good things. They believe that if the good things they do on this earth outnumber the bad things they do, then they will win God's favor. Others think that somehow everyone will get in. The Bible teaches something very different. It says that Abraham is our example for how to get to heaven. By his trust and belief in God's word, he found God's favor and blessing. We need this kind of faith. We are beginning to see in the Old Testament how God is going to rescue people from sin. Their rescue, and ours, involves faith. Faith is believing in his word.

REFLECTION AND INTERACTION

What is faith?

What does Abraham's faith tell us about how God plans to rescue people from sin?

God's Promises Extend from Abraham to Isaac and Jacob

Q. What name did God give to Abraham's family?

A. God said . . . , "Israel shall be your name." (Genesis 35:10)

Bible Reading: Genesis 35:9–15

Devotional Reading: The Promise of God
Is to Abraham, Isaac, and Jacob

God's promise about nations, and land, and kings who rule and rescue extended from Abraham to his son, whom he named Isaac. God's promise extended from Isaac to his son, whom he named Jacob. Have you ever asked your parents why they gave you your name? Maybe a special person in your family, like your grandfather or grandmother, had your name. Sometimes parents name their children after someone in the Bible. Whatever the reason, all names have something in common—they have a meaning. That's right; your name has a special meaning. In the Bible, a person's name meant something too. And if God gave someone a new name, that name usually revealed something especially important about their character. When God changed Jacob's name to *Israel*, he was keeping his promise to Abraham, Jacob's grandfather, that he would be the father of a great nation. That nation was called Israel. The character of Israel was predicted in the name *Israel*, which means "struggles with God." As we move through the big picture of God's story, we will see that much of it is about how disobedient the nation Israel is to God. They continually struggle against God, and he continues to act lovingly toward them. The Bible is a great story about God's love for a people who continually reject him.

REFLECTION AND INTERACTION

Why did your parents choose your name?

Try memorizing the big picture verse for this week: Genesis 35:10.

> **Q. What name did God give to Abraham's family?**
>
> A. God said . . . , "Israel shall be your name." (Genesis 35:10)

Bible Reading: Genesis 35:23–26

Devotional Reading: Israel's Twelve Sons Are
Later the Twelve Tribes of Israel

Do you know any families that have more than five children? More than six? Well, Israel's family had twelve boys! Imagine being one of the girls who had to put up with twelve brothers. For the rest of our time in the Old Testament, you will need to remember that the twelve sons of Israel are going to multiply and become the twelve tribes of the nation we know as Israel. The reason God blessed Israel with so many sons is because he made a promise to Abraham that he would become the father of a great nation. One of the most important things we learn about God in the Bible is that he is a promise-keeping God. When God makes a promise, he definitely keeps it. Because God was faithful to his word, he blessed Israel with twelve sons. These twelve boys would all grow up and have many sons and daughters. God was building the nation of Israel to be his people, just as he promised Abraham he would do many years before. And out of Israel would come God's forever King to rescue us.

REFLECTION AND INTERACTION

Promises are very serious things. Have you ever made a promise you didn't keep?

Why is it important that God is completely trustworthy to keep all his promises?

> **Q. What name did God give to Abraham's family?**
>
> A. God said . . . , "Israel shall be your name." (Genesis 35:10)

Bible Reading: Genesis 37:3–28

Devotional Reading: One of Israel's Sons, Joseph, Is Sold into Slavery

God works in many different ways in the world to keep his promises and make his plans succeed. We learned in our last devotional that one way God keeps his promises is by blessing certain people in different ways. But our reading today shows another way that God carries out his plans. Sometimes God carries out his plans through suffering. God knew that it would be necessary to bring Israel and his twelve sons to Egypt to protect them from a terrible famine that was coming. God can see the future, and that is one reason why his plans never fail. Joseph had not done anything wrong. He was completely innocent, yet God chose to allow him to suffer in order to save the nation of Israel from starvation. This was very important because a ruling king was promised to come from Joseph's brother, Judah (Genesis 49:10). We will all experience difficult times in our lives. During those times we need to remember that God is faithful to his promises, that he knows the future, and that his plans never fail. We have to learn to trust God, not only when he blesses us, but also when he brings suffering into our lives.

REFLECTION AND INTERACTION

What does our reading today teach us about the lengths God will go to keep his promise to rescue people from sin?

What are some ways we can prepare ourselves to trust God during tough times?

Question 13

Israel Enters Egypt

Q. What happened to Israel in Egypt?

A. [The Egyptians] set taskmasters over them. . . . But the more they were oppressed, the more they multiplied. (Exodus 1:11–12)

Bible Reading: Exodus 1:8–14

Devotional Reading: The Nation of Israel Is Large, but in Slavery

The children of Israel had been happy to come to Egypt. By sending Joseph there, God saved his newly formed nation from starvation. God's people remained in Egypt long after the famine. In fact, they remained there long after Joseph and his brothers died. God's people were fruitful and increased in number. They filled the land. By the time of our Bible reading today, they had been in Egypt for about 320 years. That's a long time! Eventually a new king came to power in Egypt. He knew nothing at all about Joseph and all the great things he had done. This king, called Pharaoh, was afraid that because the Israelites had become such a large group of people, they might want to take over the land. So Pharaoh gave orders that they should be treated as slaves, which meant they had to work very hard. The happiness of God's people turned to sadness as life became very, very difficult. But even in the hard times, God caused his people to grow and grow and grow. He was keeping his promise to Abraham, and he would rescue them at the right time.

REFLECTION AND INTERACTION

Why was Pharaoh's treatment of Abraham's descendants so wrong and harmful?

Why do you think God had his people stay in Egypt for such a long time?

Memorize this week's big picture verse: Exodus 1:11–12.

> **Q. What happened to Israel in Egypt?**
>
> A. [The Egyptians] set taskmasters over them. . . . But the more they were oppressed, the more they multiplied. (Exodus 1:11–12)

Bible Reading: Exodus 2:23–3:12

Devotional Reading: God Raises Up Moses to
Rescue Israel from Slavery in Egypt

Moses was an Israelite. He had lived in Egypt as a boy and a young man. Eventually he fled from Pharaoh and became a simple shepherd. He lived a good life, far away from all the suffering of his people in Egypt. Once, while Moses was tending his sheep, he saw the most amazing sight. A bush was on fire. As he came closer, he realized that its leaves and branches were not burning up. Suddenly, Moses heard God call to him from within the bush, "Moses! Moses!" "Here I am," Moses answered. "Do not come near," God said. "Take your sandals off your feet, for the place on which you are standing is holy ground." Moses hid his face from the burning bush because he was afraid. God told him that he had heard the cries of his people who were suffering in Egypt. He told Moses that the time had come to rescue them from slavery. Israel was a great nation now, just as God had promised Abraham hundreds of years before. God told Moses that he was sending him back to lead his people out of Egypt.

REFLECTION AND INTERACTION

What does God's plan to rescue Israel from Egypt teach you about God?

How would you feel if you had been Moses, and God chose you for such a great work?

Q. **What happened to Israel in Egypt?**

A. [The Egyptians] set taskmasters over them. . . . But the more they were oppressed, the more they multiplied. (Exodus 1:11–12)

Bible Reading: Exodus 7:1–7, 10, 13, 19–23; 8:6, 15, 17–19, 24, 32; 9:5–7, 10–12, 22–26, 34–35; 10:12–16, 20, 22–23, 27

Devotional Reading: Moses Returns to Pharaoh
with Many Signs of God's Power

Can you think of a cartoon or book character who is very, very bad? Well, the Pharaoh in Egypt wasn't a bad cartoon character; he was worse. He had no fear of God. He didn't believe in the Lord, the God of the Israelites. Pharaoh did not believe that the God of Abraham, Isaac, and Jacob was stronger than the gods of Egypt. So when Moses returned to Egypt, Pharaoh did not allow the Israelites to leave. They were his slaves. Fortunately, the Bible tells us that God had other plans. Each time Pharaoh refused to let Israel go, God sent a plague to show his great power and to punish Pharaoh and the people of Egypt for their rebellion. God sent ten plagues before Pharaoh finally got the message that God was in charge and that God's power was awesome. God is strong enough to overcome the rulers of this world. His rescue plan cannot fail.

REFLECTION AND INTERACTION

God sent ten plagues on Egypt. How many of them can you name?

What do the plagues teach you about God's intention to carry out his plans?

God Rescues Israel from Egypt

Q. What sign did God use to rescue Israel?

A. The blood shall be a sign for you. . . . And when I see the blood, I will pass over you. (Exodus 12:13)

Bible Reading: Exodus 11:1–10

Devotional Reading: The Death of Egypt's Firstborn Is a Sign of God's Power

God has a plan for the world. Even powerful human figures like Pharaoh in Egypt are not strong enough to keep God's plan from succeeding. Remember, the God of the Bible is so powerful that he created the heavens and the earth with mere words. Pharaoh doubted God's word. He doubted God's power. And even after God sent many plagues on Egypt, Pharaoh still wouldn't listen. So God demonstrated his power in a most severe way. He killed the firstborn of every Egyptian. Many people died and great sadness fell over the entire land. At last Pharaoh was forced to quit playing god and listen. We need to remember that God is all-powerful. His plans will not fail. And he will continue to judge everyone who rejects him as King even while he saves his own people.

REFLECTION AND INTERACTION

How intent is God on carrying out his big plans to rescue the world through the promises he first made to Abraham?

Begin memorizing the big picture verse for this week: Exodux 12:13.

> Q. **What sign did God use to rescue Israel?**
>
> A. The blood shall be a sign for you. . . . And when I see the blood, I will pass over you. (Exodus 12:13)

Bible Reading: Exodus 12:1–13

Devotional Reading: The Blood of the Passover
Lamb Is the Sign of God's Mercy

Sportsmen who hunt pheasants and quail often have hunting dogs. The dogs run ahead in the field until they discover where the birds are hiding. Then, they stand very still and point with their noses to let the hunters know the spot. The Bible is filled with pointers too. Passover is one of them. The blood sacrifice points to how God separates those who are getting mercy and those who are getting judgment. It points to Israel's sacrificial system as well as to Jesus, whose own blood was shed for us. In this way, with blood, God "passes over" our sins. But, we are getting ahead of ourselves. In today's reading, God provided a way out for his people if they would obey his word. They could escape the judgment of God by taking a perfect lamb, killing it, and smearing its blood over the door of their house. When the Lord saw the blood of the lamb, he "passed over" that home and did not kill its firstborn. In this way God showed mercy to Israel.

REFLECTION AND INTERACTION

How important was the blood of a sacrificial lamb in rescuing God's people?

Why do you think God refuses to have a relationship with anyone unless blood is shed as a sign that we need to have our sins forgiven?

> Q. What sign did God use to rescue Israel?
>
> A. The blood shall be a sign for you. . . . And when I see the blood, I will pass over you. (Exodus 12:13)

Bible Reading: Exodus 12:21–41

Devotional Reading: A Sign of God's Future Deliverance

What a terrifying yet true story! God's people were saved not once, but twice! First, their firstborn children were saved at Passover. Second, the entire nation was released from slavery in Egypt. They had been slaves there for over four hundred years! But God freed them from bondage. The Passover is a great picture of how God rescues his own people. Since we are all sinners, we are bound to die and be separated from God forever. We are all under his judgment. However, by starting a system where an animal dies in the place of a sinner, God showed Israel that he intended to have something (or someone) else suffer punishment for his people. How does God rescue his people? Blood will be the sign.

REFLECTION AND INTERACTION

If you were an Israelite, what would you have said to God after he had saved you?

Why is Passover such an important event in the history of Israel?

God Tells Israel How to Live as His People

> Q. What commands did God give Israel to obey?
>
> A. You shall have no other gods before me. . . . You shall not make for yourself a carved image. . . . You shall not take the name of the LORD your God in vain. . . . Remember the Sabbath day, to keep it holy. . . . Honor your father and your mother. . . . You shall not murder. You shall not commit adultery. You shall not steal. You shall not bear false witness against your neighbor. You shall not covet. . . . (Exodus 20:3–17)

Bible Reading: Deuteronomy 5:1–22

Devotional Reading: Two Aspects to Living as God's People

Have you ever seen a stage play or a concert? Perhaps you watched a Christmas concert at your church or participated in a play at school. Sometimes plays and concerts have something called an *intermission*. An intermission divides a play into two parts. It usually comes somewhere in the middle. Did you know that the Ten Commandments also has two parts? The first part (commandments 1–4) is about how to live as God's people by loving him above anyone or anything else. The second part (commandments 5–10) teaches that living as God's people means loving others as ourselves. So now we know that first, the Ten Commandments teach us what our love for God should be like, and second, they teach us how God wants us to love others.

REFLECTION AND INTERACTION

Why is it important for you to obey the words God gives in the Bible?

Sing the song "Ten Commandments" found on pages 178–79.

Take time to memorize these very important big picture verses: Exodus 20:3–17.

> **Q. What commands did God give Israel to obey?**
>
> **A.** You shall have no other gods before me. . . . You shall not make for yourself a carved image. . . . You shall not take the name of the LORD your God in vain. . . . Remember the Sabbath day, to keep it holy. . . . Honor your father and your mother. . . . You shall not murder. You shall not commit adultery. You shall not steal. You shall not bear false witness against your neighbor. You shall not covet. . . . (Exodus 20:3–17)

Bible Reading: Exodus 20:1–11

Devotional Reading: The First Four Commands
Emphasize "Love the Lord Your God"

The stage is set. God has set apart his people to be his own. He now has the undivided attention of his people, the nation of Israel. They are craving to hear God speak, and what is the first thing he says? He commands Israel to love him. Obviously, God could have said many other things first, but he didn't. God's very first words to his people show us that he wants to have a special relationship with them. He wants them to love him and not love other gods. The same is true for us. We are to love the Lord our God with all our heart, soul, strength, and mind (see Mark 12:30).

REFLECTION AND INTERACTION

What does it mean to love with all your heart, soul, strength, and mind?

Do you think Israel will be able to live as God's people? Why or why not?

> **Q. What commands did God give Israel to obey?**
>
> A. You shall have no other gods before me. . . . You shall not make for yourself a carved image. . . . You shall not take the name of the LORD your God in vain. . . . Remember the Sabbath day, to keep it holy. . . . Honor your father and your mother. . . . You shall not murder. You shall not commit adultery. You shall not steal. You shall not bear false witness against your neighbor. You shall not covet. . . . (Exodus 20:3–17)

Bible Reading: Exodus 20:12–17; Matthew 5:21–30

Devotional Reading: The Last Six Commands
Emphasize "Love Your Neighbor as Yourself"

Close your eyes for a second. Imagine that you are holding a big, red, juicy apple in your hands. Now, pretend to take a bite out of it. As you do this, imagine that the inside is all brown, mushy, and rotten. Not much fun, is it? Sometimes things can look good on the outside but be rotten on the inside. Sadly, the same was true for Israel, and is for us too. In the New Testament, when Jesus taught people how to live as God's people, he told them that God is concerned with what we look like on the *inside* as much as what we do on the *outside*. Not only should we not murder, but we should not call anyone a fool either. When Jesus talks of these six commandments, he makes it clear that living as God's people involves a *heart* that is totally committed to following God.

REFLECTION AND INTERACTION

How does our heart affect our actions?

Do you think that you can fulfill God's commands without God's Spirit?

God Sets Israel Apart to Be His People

> Q. What kind of life did God call Israel to live?
>
> A. You shall be holy to me, for I the LORD am holy and have separated you from the peoples, that you should be mine. (Leviticus 20:26)

Bible Reading: Leviticus 20:22–26; Exodus 19:1–6

Devotional Reading: God Calls Israel to Be Holy

Many people like to go camping. They travel around the country and sleep in tents and pop-up campers. Israel was familiar with camping. After three months of traveling the desert, Israel arrived at Mount Sinai. This was the place that Moses had first heard from God in the burning bush. And it will be here that God sets Israel apart to be his own people. Behind Israel were more than four hundred years of slavery. Ahead of Israel was the high calling of being God's people. The nation of Israel was to display God's character to the entire world. What a magnificent calling! They were fortunate. To be God's light in the world, they must not do deeds of darkness. They must keep from sinning against God, and instead live lives that please him. After all, God is King—and he had rescued them to set them apart to be his own people.

REFLECTION AND INTERACTION

Why was Israel to be holy?

Sing "You Are to Be Holy" found on page 181.

Begin to memorize the big picture verse for this week: Leviticus 20:26.

> Q. **What kind of life did God call Israel to live?**
>
> A. You shall be holy to me, for I the LORD am holy and have separated you from the peoples, that you should be mine. (Leviticus 20:26)

Bible Reading: Revelation 4:1–11

Devotional Reading: God Is Holy, Holy, Holy

If you could describe God in one word, what word would you choose? In the Bible God is described as having many wonderful and beautiful qualities. He is loving; he is kind; he is merciful; he is powerful; and he is many other good things. But there is one word that perhaps describes who he is better than any other. The word is *holy*. God is holy, holy, holy! God's holiness has at least two parts to it. First, *God is absolutely pure*. He is completely sinless. Second, *God is separate* from every other person and thing in the universe. God is so holy that no one even can see his face. These two things are what God required of Israel: to be absolutely pure and to be separate from the ungodly. He wants them to be different from the nations around them.

REFLECTION AND INTERACTION

Would you want to follow a god who was not holy? Why or why not?

What do you think the holiness of God meant for the nation of Israel? What should it mean for you and me?

> **Q. What kind of life did God call Israel to live?**
>
> A. You shall be holy to me, for I the LORD am holy and have separated you from the peoples, that you should be mine. (Leviticus 20:26)

Bible Reading: 1 Peter 1:13–21

Devotional Reading: The *How* and *Why* of Holiness

Do you ever get frustrated? Name some things that frustrate you. Let me give you two more. We can become frustrated when someone asks us to do something without telling us *how* to do it. And we can become frustrated when we are not told *why* we should do something. In our Bible reading today, we learn that God doesn't want us to be frustrated like that. God tells us how and why we are to follow him. He tells us how and why we are to be holy. The *how* is answered by filling our minds with thoughts that focus on the great salvation we have in Christ. We are to stay away from sin and keep our hearts filled with the hope of our reward in heaven. Of course we can't do this on our own. The Old Testament is teaching us that! Israel needed the power of the Holy Spirit—and so do we. The *why* is answered in God's very character. He is holy, so if we are his people, we are to be holy. Did you know that one day God will judge everything you have ever thought and said and done? The nation of Israel was learning the same thing after being rescued from Egypt by God. They were to be holy by keeping from sin because they were God's chosen people.

REFLECTION AND INTERACTION

Why should Israel want to be holy?

If God has told you *how* to be holy and *why* you should be holy, why is it impossible for you to be holy?

Do you see that you (like Israel) need God's Spirit?

Israel Promises to Live as God's People

Q. Did Israel promise to obey the Lord their God as King?

A. Speak to us all that the LORD our God will [say], and we will hear and do it. (Deuteronomy 5:27)

Bible Reading: Deuteronomy 5:23–27; Exodus 24:3

Devotional Reading: Israel Promises to Live as God's People

God isn't the only one who makes big promises; Israel made them too. After being rescued from Egypt, Israel had a great desire to please God, and they promised him that they would. They wanted to follow him wholeheartedly. These must have been great days! Imagine someone doing something nice for you. Let's even say that he didn't have to do it, but he did it anyway. Let's go one step further and say that he did this kind act just to show you how much he loved you. Wouldn't you want to thank him by doing anything you could for him? Of course you would. In the same way Israel wanted to thank God in any way they could for rescuing them from Egypt. Certainly, days would come, after the nearness of the rescue wore off, when Israel's true love for God would be put to the test. But on this day, everything was great! Israel promised to live as God's people.

REFLECTION AND INTERACTION

In your own words, describe what Israel is promising in today's verses.

Begin memorizing the big picture verse for this week: Deuteronomy 5:27.

Sing "I Will Have Faith in God" (p. 180), which teaches how we obey God.

> Q. Did Israel promise to obey the Lord their God as King?
>
> A. Speak to us all that the LORD our God will [say], and we will hear and do it. (Deuteronomy 5:27)

Bible Reading: Deuteronomy 8:1–10

Devotional Reading: God Exhorts His People to Keep the Law

Can you recall a teacher at school or a parent saying something like, "Listen to me. What I am saying is very important"? As you read through the Old Testament, notice how often God tells his people to listen carefully. God knew that it would be easier for Israel to *promise* to follow God than to actually *live out* that promise. We, too, must be careful to listen to God's Word. Sometimes that means making difficult choices. Sometimes it means doing the right thing rather than the thing we feel like doing. In today's passage, God reminds the Israelites that they must be careful not only to listen to him, but to do what he says. A lot depends on their obedience. Through their obedience, the world will see and know who God is and what he requires.

REFLECTION AND INTERACTION

Think of examples of when it is easy to obey God's word and other times when it is not.

How can you be more careful in listening to and following God's Word?

Q. **Did Israel promise to obey the Lord their God as King?**

A. Speak to us all that the LORD our God will [say], and we will hear and do it. (Deuteronomy 5:27)

Bible Reading: Deuteronomy 8:11–20

Devotional Reading: God Warns His People Not to Forget the Law

Sometimes when you are riding in a car, you will see a flashing light or a sign that says, "Warning! Danger Ahead." Those signs are meant to help the driver. They prepare the driver to be careful. In the verses we just read, God flashes a warning sign in front of his people—be careful that you do not forget the Lord your God or forget to obey and follow his commands. Why would God warn Israel not to forget the law so shortly after rescuing them? You probably know the answer to that question. All of us forget things very quickly, don't we? We can all remember times when we disobeyed parents or teachers shortly after they had reminded us of what is right and what is wrong. The warnings of God are good for us! We must be very careful not to forget the things that God has done for us or the commands that he has given us.

REFLECTION AND INTERACTION

Why do you think Israel needed this warning after being rescued?

Do you tend to think of a warning as a good thing or a bad thing? Why?

God Keeps All His Promises to Israel

> **Q. Did the Lord keep his promises to Israel?**
>
> A. Not one word of all the good promises that the LORD had made to the house of Israel had failed; all came to pass. (Joshua 21:45)

Bible Reading: Joshua 21:43–45

Devotional Reading: God's Promises Are Fulfilled

Have you ever waited for something for so long that you began to wonder if it would ever come? Well, the Israelites knew what it was to wait for something. Centuries before, God had promised to make Abraham into a great nation. God also promised him many descendants. On top of all that, God promised him a special land to live in. After Moses died, God used a young man named Joshua to lead God's people into the place he had promised Abraham centuries before. God's promises came true—every one of them! Abraham's descendants were now a great nation. They lived in God's chosen land, and they were poised to be a blessing to all peoples.

REFLECTION AND INTERACTION

What does this story tell you about God and his timing?

Begin memorizing the big picture verse for this week: Joshua 21:25.

Thank God for his good plans and promises and sing "God of the Promise" found on page 182.

> **Q. Did the Lord keep his promises to Israel?**
>
> **A.** Not one word of all the good promises that the LORD had made to the house of Israel had failed; all came to pass. (Joshua 21:45)

Bible Reading: 1 Kings 4:29–34; 10:23–25

Devotional Reading: God Keeps All His Promises

Have you ever played the game leapfrog? First, everyone must get in a single-file line. Then, with each person crouching down like a frog, the last person in line leaps over everyone ahead of her until she becomes the leader of the line. This leapfrogging line continues until everyone has had a chance to leap ahead of the others. Today, our Bible reading played leapfrog. We jumped ahead of some of the events in Israel's history to show that not only did God fulfill all his promises at the time of Joshua, but that those promises kept getting fulfilled in greater and greater ways. This text is so important! We cannot overstate this: Israel not only got into the Promised Land, but they became the envy of the world! King Solomon, who was David's son, ruled over Israel in the Promised Land when it was at the height of its power. Nations sought out his wisdom, and despite all the hiccups along the way, God did what he promised. The God of the Bible is a promise-keeping God! He promised Abraham that he would make him into a great nation. And he did. He promised Abraham that he would give his descendants a special place to live. And he did. We can be sure that he will keep his promise to bless all peoples of the earth through Abraham. What a great God! Israel now lives in God's place where they can worship him alone and become a blessing to all the families of the earth.

REFLECTION AND INTERACTION

What are you learning about God's love by his promise-keeping ways?

What difference does it make for you to know that God is a promise-keeping God?

> Q. **Did the Lord keep his promises to Israel?**
>
> A. Not one word of all the good promises that the LORD had made to the house of Israel had failed; all came to pass. (Joshua 21:45)

Bible Reading: Joshua 23:1–5, 14–16

Devotional Reading: God Is Faithful to His Promises

Having leapt ahead last time to show the full measure of the promises God kept to Israel, today we backtrack to the close of Joshua's life. Sometimes when hikers climb a mountain, they look ahead to see what is coming, then backtrack along the trail. They return to their starting place and regroup before going on. Today, we regroup. We backtrack our way until we reach Joshua again. Joshua did many great things in his life. But most importantly, at the close of his life he wanted to remind the people how good God had been to them. As an old man, he told Israel about all the wonderful promises God had kept. He told them to remember how good God had been to them. Joshua was a humble man who knew what was important in life: honoring God and praising and thanking him for keeping all his promises. Joshua was happy to be one of God's people living in God's place, and he didn't want anything to ruin those blessings for those who would come after him.

REFLECTION AND INTERACTION

How can you be a thankful person, someone who honors God?

Name some ways that God showed his love toward Israel during Joshua's lifetime.

God Begins His Promise

Review 1: Reviewing the Memory Verses

Don't forget that one way you can help your child(ren) learn is to memorize the big picture verses of God's Word *with* them. In fact, Psalm 1 tells us that the person blessed by God is one whose "delight is in the law of the LORD, and on his law he meditates day and night" (v. 2). If you and your child(ren) commit to memorizing all the big picture verses in this devotional, you will have helped them and yourself be able to put the storyline of the Bible together.

Take time this week to plant God's Word in your heart. Review the memory verses for the past nine weeks. Can you say all eighteen?

Review 2: Reviewing the Big Picture

One of the unique features of this devotional is that it emphasizes the big picture of the Bible rather than isolated Bible stories outside of their progressive context. At this point in the devotional, some of the connections in the Bible's storyline should be evident. For instance:

First Ten Weeks

1. God creates a place (Eden) and a people (Adam and Eve) and rules them by his word.
2. In rejecting God's word, God's people lose their place.
3. All people reject God's word, are set apart for judgment, and are punished (flood).

Second Ten Weeks

1. God promises (to Abraham) to establish a new people who will live in a specific place.
2. God keeps his word and establishes a people (Israel) and gives them a place (Promised Land).
3. Israel accepts God's word and is set apart for God and is a blessing to all peoples.

Are you beginning to see the progression and continuity of these themes?

Take some time this week to talk about the connections between the two ten-week segments.

Review 3: Learning by the Socratic Method

The Socratic method is a learning method taken from the ancient teacher Socrates. He had a unique way of teaching his pupils: he would simply ask perceptive questions, and discussion would follow. To inspire such discussion is one of the reasons we included the reflection and interaction sections for each day. By asking a few simple questions, good discussions can begin that allow you the chance to teach your children. Not only that, but such questions allow you to see how much your children are comprehending from the studies.

Go back over the devotional readings of this week. Try to think of a question or two that will stimulate dialogue with your kids about something they learned.

PART 3

God Continues His Promise

Questions 19–27

Israel Rejects God as King

Q. Did Israel keep their promises to the LORD?

A. The LORD said . . . , "They have rejected me from being king over them." (1 Samuel 8:7)

Bible Reading: 1 Samuel 8:4–9

Devotional Reading: Israel Rejects God as King

If you wanted to jump twenty-five feet into the air, could you? If you wanted to run one hundred miles per hour, could you? If you wanted to grow up to be twelve feet tall, could you? Now, think about one more question: If Israel wanted to keep their promises to God and follow him as their king, could they? No, the sad fact is they could not. Just wanting to do something didn't somehow give them magical abilities to do it. The problem with Israel is the same problem all of Adam's descendants have. We are sinners. Our hearts are bent toward disobedience. We should not be shocked by Israel's rejection of God as King. To know the extent of their rebellion, we only need to look at our own hearts. Their desire for an earthly king is evidence that they are breaking their promises.

REFLECTION AND INTERACTION

What is the history of Israel in the Old Testament teaching you about all of us, about human nature?

Do you think that people are basically good or evil? Can we fix the problem or do we need rescuing?

Begin to memorize this week's big picture verse: 1 Samuel 8:7.

Q. Did Israel keep their promises to the LORD?

A. The LORD said . . . , "They have rejected me from being king over them." (1 Samuel 8:7)

Bible Reading: Deuteronomy 31:14–18; Joshua 24:16–20; Judges 21:25

Devotional Reading: God Knew Israel Would Reject Him as King

Imagine you had a dog that you loved. You took great care of it: you fed it good food, you took it for long walks, and you played with it every day after school. Now imagine the dog ran away and went to live at the neighbor's house down the street. How do you think that would make you feel? You would feel very sad. Something like that happens in the Bible. The promise-keeping God of the Bible—the God who put his people in a very special place so that he could have a relationship with them and bless all families of the earth through them, will be told by Israel that they no longer love him. Israel rejects God's love. This is something Joshua knew was going to happen. He had been with Moses when God foretold this to them. And sure enough, after Joshua dies, the people begin doing what is right in their own eyes rather than what God commanded. They become rebels who have dethroned God as King.

REFLECTION AND INTERACTION

What do you think it was like to live during this time in Israel's history?

Do you ever reject God as King in the way you act?

Q. Did Israel keep their promises to the LORD?

A. The LORD said . . . , "They have rejected me from being king over them." (1 Samuel 8:7)

Bible Reading: 1 Kings 4:20–26; 11:1–3

Devotional Reading: Looking Forward—God Knew
Israel's Kings Would Reject His Word

Do you remember reading from 1 Kings 4 a couple of weeks ago? It was when we played leapfrog. We looked at it then when summarizing Israel at the height of its powers. Today, we want to do something similar. We want to jump ahead in the Bible story to see that even in the seemingly good times, Israel's rejection of God's word was beginning to pop up. But instead of playing leapfrog, pretend you are looking through a set of binoculars that allow you to see far beyond the time of Joshua's prophecy to the time when Israel is ruled by King Solomon. Our Bible reading *seems* to say that everything is great. But it isn't. Verse 26 says that Solomon had "40,000 stalls of horses for his chariots, and 12,000 horsemen." Having so many horses is the very thing God said the king was not do (see Deuteronomy 17:16)! Solomon also married foreign women, which God had forbidden (Exodus 23:31–33). What an irony: the seeds of the decline of Israel are present even in the great King Solomon, who ruled Israel when it was flying high.

REFLECTION AND INTERACTION

Are you beginning to see that *God* must have hidden plans to rescue all peoples from sin?

Why is it important that we see what King Solomon was doing against God?

God Is Not Surprised

Q. How was God's rule over Israel restored?

A. They anointed David king over Israel. (2 Samuel 5:3)

Bible Reading: 1 Samuel 16:1–13

Devotional Reading: God Was Not Taken by Surprise

When was the last time you were really surprised? Did you know that God is never surprised? God knew that Israel would break their promises. He knew that they would ask for an earthly king. Although this meant that they were rejecting him as their ruler, God, in his mercy, had already planned to give them a king who would foreshadow his promise of rescue. After the death of King Saul, God gave Israel a king who would be a godly example to them. Would this next king be tall and powerful like Saul? Samuel certainly thought so. However, God had a different idea. He wanted a ruler who loved him more than anything else in the world. When God chose the next king of Israel, he picked a shepherd boy named David, not because he was great and strong, but because he had a great and strong heart for God. God's promises were still in place!

REFLECTION AND INTERACTION

Who did God chose to be king over Israel? Why did he choose David?

What does this teach you about God's plans and promises to rescue his people?

Memorize the big picture verse for this week: 2 Samuel 5:3.

> **Q. How was God's rule over Israel restored?**
>
> A. They anointed David king over Israel. (2 Samuel 5:3)

Bible Reading: 1 Samuel 17:1–10, 32–54

Devotional Reading: God Chooses David as King

Suppose two people were going to fight. One was a giant—tall, strong, and massive. The other was a young boy who spent his time watching sheep. The giant had huge weapons and armor. The boy had only a few stones and a sling. Who do you think would win? The obvious answer is the giant. But in the story of David and Goliath, the boy wins! David won because he had more than just stones and a sling. He had the living God on his side. God wants us to learn a very important lesson through this story. God wants us to know that he fully intends to rescue his people from their enemies. He will overcome those who reject God. He will establish a people who follow him. God still cares for his people and has plans to rescue them completely. And he will do it by establishing his own King! Remember, this was in God's plans all along (see Genesis 35:11; 49:10, and question 12).

REFLECTION AND INTERACTION

What do you learn about God from the story of David and Goliath?

Thank God for raising up someone to rescue his people even after they continually reject him.

> Q. **How was God's rule over Israel restored?**
>
> A. They anointed David king over Israel. (2 Samuel 5:3)

Bible Reading: 1 Chronicles 18:1–8, 14

Devotional Reading: David Reigns as King

Sometime after defeating Goliath, David became king over Israel, all according to God's plan. As king, David continued to conquer and rule over God's enemies. Many mighty foes challenged him in battle, but they always fell at David's feet. Do you have any idea why his reign was so successful? The answer is simple: *God was with him*. David administered justice and righteousness to all the people. David was a great king, and God was using him to show his people what God is really like. King David is an important part of understanding the big picture of the storyline of the Bible. God's promise to bruise Satan's head through Eve's offspring, and his promise to bless all the peoples of the earth through Abraham, were going forward in the person of King David.

REFLECTION AND INTERACTION

What do you think made David a great king for Israel?

What was God teaching Israel through David's rule? What is he teaching you?

God Promises a New King

> **Q. Did God say his promise was fulfilled when David became king?**
>
> A. I will raise up your offspring after you . . . and I will establish his kingdom. (2 Samuel 7:12)

Bible Reading: 2 Samuel 7:8–13, 18–26

Devotional Reading: God's Promises David a Forever Kingdom!

Have you ever done something nice for someone only to have her do something even nicer for you in return? It's fun when that happens, isn't it? Did you know that happened to King David? God had been good to him, and when Israel became a great nation, David wanted to do something nice for God. He wanted to build him a temple. But David learned that you cannot outdo God in doing nice things for others. God told David that he had a better gift in store for him. He planned to make David's kingdom last *forever*. God was going to bring a King into the world who would rule a forever kingdom—and this King would come from David's line. Imagine how excited David must have been to hear this news. God's rescue plan involved more than God's promises to Abraham, Isaac, and Jacob, and more than the ministry of Moses. God promised David that his rescue plan involved one of David's own descendants, who would rule God's kingdom people forever. What a wonderful promise!

REFLECTION AND INTERACTION

What kind of king would it take to rule over a forever kingdom?

Sing "Forever Kingdom" found on page 183.

Begin to memorize this week's big picture verse: 2 Samuel 7:12.

> **Q. Did God say his promise was fulfilled when David became king?**
>
> A. I will raise up your offspring after you . . . and I will establish his kingdom. (2 Samuel 7:12)

Bible Reading: Psalm 110:1; Matthew 22:41–46

Devotional Reading: David Knew That the Coming
King Would Be Greater Than He Was

With the help of God's Spirit, King David came to understand what God's promise to him meant. He knew that one of his descendants would make God's name great. In fact, this future King would be *greater than David*. Now, put your thinking cap on, because what you are about to hear is hard to understand. When we read King David referring to somebody else as *Lord*, we learn that King David, the "lord of Israel," had a Lord who is greater than he. Imagine that! The lord of Israel calls someone else his Lord and King. Who do you think that might be? In the New Testament, Jesus helped the teachers of his own day understand this strange truth because even they had a hard time getting it. Jesus knew that the people of his own day wanted the days of David to return. They thought he was the greatest king. But Jesus told them that even David knew there was going to be a *future* king who would be the greatest of all. In fact, Jesus knew more than this—he knew that he was the promised King whom God sent into the world to rescue us from sin and rule over us forever!

REFLECTION AND INTERACTION

Why might David, lord and ruler of Israel, call another person his Lord?

Jesus views himself as the King of kings and Lord of lords. If this is true, how should you think and respond to Jesus?

Q. **Did God say his promise was fulfilled when David became king?**

A. I will raise up your offspring after you . . . and I will establish his kingdom. (2 Samuel 7:12)

Bible Reading: Acts 2:22–36

Devotional Reading: The Apostles Proclaimed That Jesus Is the King That David Pointed To

Today we are jumping ahead in the Bible story to the book of Acts. In Acts, Peter, one of the apostles, preaches a great sermon. He helps the people of his own day understand that Jesus of Nazareth must be *the* Lord if he is King David's Lord. He explains to the crowd (and to us) that Jesus is actually the Messiah King that David had called Lord. David had written how the Messiah, or Christ, would be raised from the dead. And since this Jesus of Nazareth was indeed raised from the dead, he is the Lord that Israel should be looking for! In other words, Jesus is the descendant of David who is the Lord, the King, the ruler over God's people and God's forever kingdom. He is the one who will bless all the families of the earth.

REFLECTION AND INTERACTION

Skim over the genealogy of Jesus in Matthew 1. How does Matthew point out that Jesus is David's son?

Are you surprised that God kept his promises by the death and resurrection of his Son?

God Promises a New Place

> Q. **Did Solomon say God's promise was fulfilled when the temple was built?**
>
> A. The highest heaven cannot contain you; how much less this house that I have built! (1 Kings 8:27)

Bible Reading: 2 Chronicles 6:1–11; 7:11–18

Devotional Reading: The Temple Was God's Place of Dwelling among His People

Some people get to work in construction and build things. That is fun but hard work. Do you recall that David wanted to construct something nice for God? He wanted to build God a temple (or house). Well, his son Solomon was the one who actually got to build that temple. Now, God doesn't need a house to live in, because he is spirit and lives above all creation, but that doesn't mean that Solomon's temple wouldn't have God's blessing. Far from it: God wanted the temple built. He wanted it as a visible sign. He wanted his people to see that he lived among them—that he had a place with them. Solomon's temple represented the place of God. It meant that God lived with his people. And when Solomon finished it, God filled it with his glory for all the people to see. How exciting! God was once again dwelling with his people in the special place he had provided for them.

REFLECTION AND INTERACTION

What purpose did the temple serve in Israel?

Begin memorizing this week's big picture verse: 1 Kings 8:27.

> Q. **Did Solomon say God's promise was fulfilled when the temple was built?**
>
> A. The highest heaven cannot contain you; how much less this house that I have built! (1 Kings 8:27)

Bible Reading: Deuteronomy 12:5–14; 2 Chronicles 7:12

Devotional Reading: The Temple Was God's Place
of Provision for the Sins of His People

In our last devotional reading, we learned about the temple. Do you remember who built it? Solomon did. Can you remember God's purpose for the temple? It was a visible sign of God living among his people. In our Bible reading today, we see that the temple was also to be the place where God's people would offer sacrifices for sin. Because the temple was a place for people to seek God's forgiveness, it became a very important place. Jerusalem, the city where the temple was located, was the center for Jewish life and religion. In the coming weeks, we will read about the ultimate sacrifice God made for his people. For now, remember this about the temple: it was the place God provided for animal sacrifices to be carried out. It was the place where people came in faith for the forgiveness of sin. This practice of sacrificing animals for sin went all the way back to Moses. Do you remember the Passover lamb and the sacrificial system God put in place? Well, the temple of Solomon became not only the sign of God living among his people, but also the place where the sacrifices of a sinful people were made in the presence of a holy and forgiving God.

REFLECTION AND INTERACTION

Where did God want people to seek him? Why did he give them a special place to sacrifice?

What is sin? Why do God's people need forgiveness?

> Q. Did Solomon say God's promise was fulfilled when the temple was built?
>
> A. The highest heaven cannot contain you; how much less this house that I have built! (1 Kings 8:27)

Bible Reading: John 1:1–3, 14–18; 2:13–22; Hebrews 10:19–22

Devotional Reading: Jesus Is the Temple

Today in our reading we fly over lots of ground to a place further along in the storyline of the Bible. With the coming of Jesus of Nazareth, the Old Testament way of paying for sins changed. In our Bible reading today, John tells us that Jesus is God's temple. The word in John 1:14 that is translated "dwelt" really means "tabernacled." The tabernacle is what God's people had in the time of Moses prior to Solomon's temple. In other words, John is teaching us that Jesus is the visible sign of God living among his people! He is God's *place*. Therefore, Jesus is replacing the tabernacle and the temple with himself. So then, to find God's presence in the world, we must look to Jesus. From the book of Hebrews we learn that Jesus is the sacrifice that takes away the sins of the world. If you are looking for forgiveness for sin, you must look to Jesus. He is both the *place* of God among his people, and the *provision* of God for the sins of his people.

REFLECTION AND INTERACTION

How does the New Testament help us understand the Old Testament?

Thank God for making the storyline of the Bible clear.

The Kings of the Earth Reject God's Promises

Q. How did the nations respond to God's promise?

A. The kings of the earth set themselves, and the rulers take counsel together, against the LORD and against his Anointed. (Psalm 2:2)

Bible Reading: Psalm 2:1–3

Devotional Reading: The Kings of the Earth Reject God as King

I'll bet that learning about earthly kings who reject God's plans for a new King comes as no surprise to you, does it? The Old Testament is filled with people, all peoples in fact, who reject God. Our Bible reading today tells a story we have heard before. People on earth are rejecting God and his promises to install a new King who will rule over the nations forever. Our memory verse for this week is found in verse 2 of this psalm: "The kings of the earth set themselves, and the rulers take counsel together, against the LORD and against his Anointed." The nations will always reject God's king, whether it be Solomon or David, or as we will learn next time, Jesus of Nazareth, God's forever King.

REFLECTION AND INTERACTION

Think of some ways that you reject God and his King. What should you do?

This week's verse is a summary of how people treat God's rescue plan. Take time to memorize Psalm 2:2.

Q. How did the nations respond to God's promise?

A. The kings of the earth set themselves, and the rulers take counsel together, against the LORD and against his Anointed. (Psalm 2:2)

Bible Reading: Psalm 2:1–9; Acts 4:25–28

Devotional Reading: God's Plan to Establish His King Succeeds Anyway

Close your eyes for a minute. Imagine that you are in a magic time machine. It can take you forward in time hundreds and hundreds of years in seconds. Are you buckled up and ready to go? Okay, open your eyes. Would you want to go in the magic time machine or would it be too scary? Our Bible reading today is like going in a time machine. When we read from the book of Acts, we speed ahead hundreds and hundreds of years to the time just after Jesus was crucified and raised from the dead. The apostle Peter quotes our memory verse in his sermon. He tells his listeners (and us) that when David wrote of kings rejecting the Lord, he was referring specifically to King Herod and Pilate. And in fact, Psalm 2 refers to the whole world who rejects Jesus of Nazareth as God's King! But Peter also knew that God was laughing in heaven because he fulfilled his promise to make Jesus King anyway! Jesus's death and resurrection is the big picture behind God's rescue plan. Jesus is God's King who rules over God's people.

REFLECTION AND INTERACTION

How do these two passages increase your confidence in the Bible as being God's Word?

Do you think anything can stop God's plan to rescue representatives from all families of the earth from sin?

Q. How did the nations respond to God's promise?

A. The kings of the earth set themselves, and the rulers take counsel together, against the LORD and against his Anointed. (Psalm 2:2)

Bible Reading: Psalm 2:10–12

Devotional Reading: Responding to God's Plan

When riding in the car, do you ever notice the yellow signs along the road? Sometimes they have words on them, and other times just drawings. Do you know what yellow signs mean? They mean "warning." Warning signs are important for drivers. They help drivers know that they need to be looking out for something just ahead. The Bible reading today is like a big yellow warning sign. It tells us to be careful not to be like those who reject Jesus, God's King. "Be wise," it says, and "serve the LORD." We are to love him lest he be angry with us and judge us. How great God is for telling us what to do now that he has set up Jesus as King over all things! Remember, his coming again in judgment is just ahead—and he will punish everyone who rejects him as King.

REFLECTION AND INTERACTION

What do the warning signs in the Bible teach you about God?

What would it mean for you to submit to Jesus as King?

The Kings of Israel Reject God's Promises

Q. What did God say about Israel's response to his promise?

A. Children have I reared and brought up, but they have rebelled against me. (Isaiah 1:2)

Bible Reading: Isaiah 1:1–4

Devotional Reading: The Writing Prophets
Show Israel's Rejection of God

What is God doing with Israel in the Bible? Think about the story we have heard so far: God took the nation of Israel, which started just as a tiny family, and helped them grow into a great nation of many children. He gave them a king, and all the families of the earth wondered at their wisdom and greatness. However, even the kings David and Solomon disobeyed God. Certainly they didn't sound like the rescuing King God had promised; that King must not have entered the story yet. God sent prophets like Isaiah to discipline God's disobedient children. According to verse 1 in our Bible reading, Isaiah prophesied against Israel in the days of kings Uzziah, Jotham, Ahaz, and Hezekiah. About King Ahaz, the Bible says, "He did not do what was right in the eyes of the LORD" (2 Kings 16:2). The kings of Israel rejected God's promises. God's children rebelled against him. So God used prophets like Isaiah to tell the people that God was calling on the heavens and the earth to be witnesses of their rebellion. God warned that he was going to force them out of the land and into exile, just as he had forced Adam and Eve out of the garden long before them.

REFLECTION AND INTERACTION

Why do you think so much of the Old Testament deals with people's disobedience toward God, even after his many rescues?

In what ways are you like Israel when it comes to following God's instructions? How are you different?

Memorize this week's big picture verse: Isaiah 1:2.

> **Q. What did God say about Israel's response to his promise?**
>
> **A.** Children have I reared and brought up, but they have rebelled against me. (Isaiah 1:2)

Bible Reading: 1 Kings 18:16–40

Devotional Reading: The Nonwriting Prophets Show Israel's Rejection of God

Elijah was a great prophet, second only to Moses in the whole Old Testament. He spoke for God to kings who rejected him. Ahab was one such king. He ruled over God's people but served idols. Elijah was angry when the kings of God's people rejected God, so he challenged Ahab, and his idols, to a contest. Elijah easily won because he followed the living and true God. The other gods were not really gods at all. The kings of God's people should have known better than to serve idols, but they did it anyway. The entire record of the Bible is in agreement: the kings of Israel rejected God's promises. They served other gods—and the result, as we will see next week, is that they will forfeit the land, the place, that God had given them.

REFLECTION AND INTERACTION

Do you think seeing this amazing miracle at Mount Carmel changed Israel's mind about worshiping the true God? Do you think it changed their hearts?

Why is it important to read about what the prophets did and said?

> Q. **What did God say about Israel's response to his promise?**
>
> A. Children have I reared and brought up, but they have rebelled against me. (Isaiah 1:2)

Bible Reading: 1 Kings 11:42–12:17

Devotional Reading: Israel Is Divided into Two Places and Two Kings

It is painful when a nation is ripped in two, and that is what happened to Israel. When King Solomon died, a united Israel died as well. Solomon's son Rehoboam became king, but he was arrogant and ungodly, so many Israelites did not follow him. They chose Jeroboam as king instead, but he was ungodly too. So the land, the place promised to Abraham that the Lord had given them, was divided in two. Ten tribes followed Jeroboam, leaving only two with Rehoboam. The ten tribes kept the name *Israel* and lived in the northern part of the country. The two tribes took the name *Judah* and stayed in the south. What a terrible time it must have been, when God's people no longer lived under God's word, and no longer lived together. Do you know what the saddest thing about all this is? The worst is still to come. Israel, once great in the world, will soon be forced out of the land altogether. God will not dwell with sinful people. He will withdraw his hand of blessing from them. His glory will depart.

REFLECTION AND INTERACTION

What does Israel's rejection of God teach you about our ability to follow God?

What are some of the devastating effects of disobedience?

Israel Enters Exile

Q. How did the Lord God judge his people this time?

A. Therefore my people [will] go into exile. (Isaiah 5:13)

Bible Reading: Isaiah 5:1–2, 7–13

Devotional Reading: God's People and Their
Promised Land Are under God's Judgment

Do you like gardening? Planting flowers or vegetables can be hard work, but it can also be very rewarding. There is something special about watching a plant that you planted grow. You water it, feed it, and wait. Finally you get the pleasure of seeing blossoms burst forth, and tomatoes ripen on the vine. How maddening it would be if only weeds flourished where flowers were to grow. Or the land where tomatoes ought to be remained dry and barren. Something like this happened when God planted Israel in the Promised Land. He looked for fruit and fullness and found only bad fruit and barren land. As a result of the sins of his people, God forces his people out of the place he had given them. He sent them into exile. They had to leave, just as Adam and Eve had to leave the garden.

REFLECTION AND INTERACTION

From our Bible reading, how would you describe God's care for his people?

Our verse for this week is a sad one. Do you know why?

Begin to memorize this week's verse: Isaiah 5:13.

> **Q. How did the Lord God judge his people this time?**
>
> A. Therefore my people [will] go into exile. (Isaiah 5:13)

Bible Reading: 2 Kings 17:5–18

Devotional Reading: The Ten Tribes of Israel Are Forced into Exile

Nobody enjoys being the bearer of bad news. It's not any fun. When we read the Bible, we are usually looking for the good news, but today the writer has only bad things to tell us. They are not easy things to hear, but they are things we need to know. Israel, the ten tribes to the north, went into exile in 722 BC. That is, about seven hundred years before Jesus came, they were sent out of the Promised Land. They were totally wiped off the face of the earth and never heard from again. They disobeyed God in almost every way imaginable—and they paid for it with their lives. The Lord God, who through Abraham called out a great nation, complete with its own land and kings, is now forced to judge them for their sin.

REFLECTION AND INTERACTION

What does the seriousness of God's judgment teach you about God?

What does it teach you about your ability to obey God?

> Q. How did the Lord God judge his people this time?
>
> A. Therefore my people [will] go into exile. (Isaiah 5:13)

Bible Reading: Lamentations 1:1–5

Devotional Reading: The Two Tribes of Judah Are Forced into Exile

Jeremiah is sometimes referred to as the weeping prophet. He cried many tears over the fall of Judah. He wept bitterly over its sins. Jeremiah wrote the book of Lamentations, from which we took today's Bible reading. Lamentations includes four poems (called *laments*) and a prayer. Jeremiah was a godly and great prophet. He longed to see Judah obey God—to remain his people, living in his place, under his rule—but it was not to be. God told Jeremiah that the sins of Judah were engraved on their hearts with an iron tool (Jeremiah 17:1). In other words, the hearts of the people of Judah were like cold stone toward God. Judah was forced into exile around 586 BC, roughly 135 years after the northern tribes were taken by Assyria. Remember, though, that God's promise to bless all the families of the earth continued, and those promises involved Judah (Genesis 49:10)! God will bring his forever King from the tiny group of people who went into exile at the time of Jeremiah. God's plan to rescue a people for himself does not depend on Israel's ability to stay in the land by following him. In fact, what the Old Testament teaches us is that God's plan to rescue us is going to come about because of, and only because of, God's faithfulness to his own word!

REFLECTION AND INTERACTION

Thank God for his faithfulness to his word.

Ask God for forgiveness for your unfaithfulness to his word.

The Ragged Return of Israel from Exile

> Q. Did God promise to rescue his people from exile?
>
> A. I will bring you back to the place from which I sent you into exile. (Jeremiah 29:14)

Bible Reading: Jeremiah 29:1, 4, 7–14

Devotional Reading: A Prophet's Letter Gives
Hope to God's People in Exile

Most people love getting mail. Receiving letters from friends and family who live far away is exciting. I think that when the people living far away in exile received Jeremiah's short letter, they couldn't wait to hear what it said. I can almost see the crowds gathering to hear it be read aloud. Cheers of joy probably erupted after they heard it. Jeremiah had good news from God. Israel would be in exile seventy years, then return to the Promised Land. God was not finished with them! He had plans for them, plans to prosper them and not harm them. Hope returned to the downcast people. Prayers of thanksgiving replaced conversations of regret. Once again they could believe that God's promise was continuing! He still planned to dwell with his people and bless all the families of the earth through them.

REFLECTION AND INTERACTION

Why is our verse for this week a gracious one? Begin to memorize Jeremiah 29:14.

From our Bible reading, how would you describe God's care for his people?

Q. Did God promise to rescue his people from exile?

A. I will bring you back to the place from which I sent you into exile. (Jeremiah 29:14)

Bible Reading: Ezra 3:7–13

Devotional Reading: God's People Return to Jerusalem,
and Zerubbabel Rebuilds the Temple, But . . .

What a time to have been alive. What if you were one of those who got to return to Jerusalem after seventy years of exile? God brought his people back into the Promised Land. The books of Ezra, Nehemiah, Esther, and Haggai speak of it. A man named Zerubbabel was one of the men in charge of rebuilding the temple. He got the job done with the help of many others. What a great time of celebration! But did you notice that many of the people, those who had seen the glory days of Judah prior to the exile, were now old men? These people wept. They knew that this temple was far less grand than the one that Solomon built. Although getting back into the land is an accomplishment, we learn that Israel as a nation will not regain the prominence and stature it had during the days of kings David and Solomon. However, rebuilding the temple is still important. It was the only visible sign, or way of preaching to the world, that God's promises were continuing. God dwells on earth. He lives among people. And he still plans to bless all peoples.

REFLECTION AND INTERACTION

What does the return, the ragged return, of Israel teach you about God?

Take time to thank God for his continuing work in your life.

> Q. **Did God promise to rescue his people from exile?**
>
> A. I will bring you back to the place from which I sent you into exile. (Jeremiah 29:14)

Bible Reading: Nehemiah 13:15, 19–27

Devotional Reading: The Ragged Behavior of God's People

Something that is ragged has lost its newness. It is no longer crisp and clean. I suppose that is where the word *rags* come from. Rags are good for something, but not much. We have learned in our Bible reading today that Israel's return to the Promised Land was a ragged one. Good for something, but not much. The people still sinned against God. They worked on the Sabbath. They married foreign women. Nehemiah, who was one of the other men in charge of rebuilding Jerusalem, got so angry at these sins that he literally pulled the hair out of people's heads! He knew that God's people would not be able to stay pure. They were no longer clean. The people who returned to Jerusalem were a ragged bunch. This teaches us that we must look elsewhere for the fulfillment of God's promises. We must look for an Israel whose heart is pure, clean, and spotless. For God to bless all peoples through Israel, we must find an Israel, or at a minimum *one* Israelite, whose heart is crisp and clean toward God. And for that, we must look forward to Jesus.

REFLECTION AND INTERACTION

What does the behavior of God's people teach you about the extent of your heart problem?

What is amazing about God's treatment of these ragged exiles?

God Promises a New People

> **Q.** How will God make it possible for his people to follow him as King?
>
> **A.** I will give you a new heart, and a new spirit I will put within you. (Ezekiel 36:26)

Bible Reading: Ezekiel 36:22–32

Devotional Reading: God's Promise, for His Own Glory, Is Repeated

Has anyone ever made you a promise that you were excited about? In our Bible reading today God continues to give his people the best promise ever. He promises them a new heart and a new spirit. The Israelites, even after returning from exile into their land, needed this encouragement. Life would not always be as it was. God was going to do something spectacular for them. Not only does God promise a heart and spirit that follow him, but we see how God will do this—through the Holy Spirit. The Holy Spirit will change people from the inside out. He will give them new life; they will be new people (Ezekiel 37). What a promise! When God gave this promise, it wasn't because of anything that the Israelites did—they certainly didn't deserve a new heart. God gave them this promise for his own glory. In his rescue, everyone, everywhere, will see how great God is!

REFLECTION AND INTERACTION

How can you tell if you have a heart that is hard like stone?

Does God give new hearts today?

Memorize this week's big picture verse: Ezekiel 36:26.

> Q. How will God make it possible for his people to follow him as King?
>
> A. I will give you a new heart, and a new spirit I will put within you. (Ezekiel 36:26)

Bible Reading: Joel 2:28–32

Devotional Reading: Even Preexilic Prophets
Said God's Promise Was Continuing

God's continuing promise is not a commitment he made just once to Israel. We find his promise all over the Old Testament. Joel was a prophet who lived before the exile, yet even he speaks of the day when God's Spirit will be poured out on all people! The promise of God is real; it is fresh; it is hinted at throughout all of Scripture. Therefore, we should ask: "Is there a point in history, after the exile, when God's promise to pour out his Spirit comes true?" The New Testament says, "Yes!" The pouring out of God's Spirit came with Jesus's life, death, and resurrection. The Holy Spirit rested on Jesus at his baptism. He gave Jesus his power throughout his life and ministry. God is with his people in the person of Jesus. After Christ ascended back into heaven, God sent the Holy Spirit, who lives in all who believe in him. God changes people, through the power of the Holy Spirit, to follow him.

REFLECTION AND INTERACTION

Do you see the connection between how God saves us and the ministry of the Holy Spirit?

What do God's continuing promises teach you about God?

> Q. How will God make it possible for his people to follow him as King?
>
> A. I will give you a new heart, and a new spirit I will put within you. (Ezekiel 36:26)

Bible Reading: Malachi 4:1–6

Devotional Reading: Old Testament Ending—The Promise Is Coming!

What is the weather like in the spring? The world around you starts to get warmer as the sunlight gets stronger, but sometimes it is still chilly, especially in the shade. Summer with all its warmth has not yet arrived. As the Old Testament ends, Israel is chilly. They are in the shade, unable to move into the light where it is warmer. But that's okay: Malachi, a postexilic prophet, essentially says, "The day is coming! God's promise is continuing! Those who revere his name will soon find the sun of righteousness rise upon them with healing in its wings. On that day the people will leap in the fields like young, excited calves!" The Old Testament closes with a final hint about when this will be. Malachi 4:5 says that one like Elijah will come first. He will turn the hearts of the fathers toward their children and the hearts of the children toward their fathers. Jesus said that John the Baptist is the Elijah this verse speaks of—which means that Jesus ushers in the day of the Lord! Get ready! God will fulfill his promises!

REFLECTION AND INTERACTION

Recall some of the things you learned from our study of the Old Testament. How faithful is God in fulfilling his promises?

Spend some time praising God for his faithfulness.

God Continues His Promise

Review 1: The Plotline of God's Promise Continues

Isn't the Old Testament a rich and wonderful collection of books? It opens with the stunning and panoramic views of universal history in Genesis 1–11. Thousands and thousands of years are covered in a few brief chapters! We called this part "God Creates His Kingdom." But just when you think the emphasis of Genesis is going to be about universal things, it quickly shifts gears at chapter 12 to speak of one man, Abraham. The remainder of Genesis, chapters 12–50, is generally unconcerned with universal history. Instead, it follows the history of one family. The irony, of course, is that while the Bible opens with universal history and then moves to patriarchal history, we learn that this family history will have universal implications. Everything after Genesis 11 has a bearing on where history is heading! We called part 2 "God Begins His Promise." In part 2 we traced how the promises of God to one man came to fulfillment with the nation of Israel, in the Promised Land, under kings David and Solomon. Finally, we saw Israel's failure and exile. But in the downturn of Israel we learned that God's promises to rescue the world from sin are wholly dependent on *him* keeping his promises, not on whether Israel keeps theirs. We titled part 3 "God Continues His Promise."

Are you beginning to get a grasp of the Bible's storyline? Sit down this week and talk about the logic and symmetry of the Old Testament.

Review 2: Reviewing the Big Picture Verses

At this point in the devotional both you and your children are looking for some closure. You have been at this for a while! Perhaps you fell behind on the memory work. Pick up wherever you left off and use this week to put it all together. Maybe it will take longer than this week. That's okay; just stay at it. You might also use this week to review some of your children's favorite songs. Music is the language of the soul, and the songs are another way to reinforce what you have been learning these past months.

Review 3: The Family at Conversation

Thirty weeks is a long time! You've made it through the Old Testament. We hope that you are more convinced than ever of the benefit of family devotions, especially devotions that help you and your kids get a better grasp on the storyline of the Bible. Keep up the conversations with your kids about the Bible! A family engaging in conversation is a healthy sign. If you have been memorizing the big picture verses, then you will be excited to learn that you are only eighteen away from telling the entire storyline of the Bible through memorizing the forty-five big picture verses. We especially hope that you are more convinced than ever the Bible's words are God's very own words!

PART 4

Jesus Fulfills God's Promise

Questions 28–36

Jesus Is Born

Q. How did the angel introduce Jesus as God's promised King?

A. I bring you good news of a great joy that will be for all the people. For unto you is born this day in the city of David a Savior, who is Christ the Lord. (Luke 2:10–11)

Bible Reading: Luke 2:1–7

Devotional Reading: Mary Gives Birth to the Promised One

Of all the exciting moments in time, one of the most exciting is when a baby is born. I bet that there is a great story to tell about the day you were born! Perhaps you were born in the middle of the night or during a winter snowstorm. Maybe your arrival caught your parents by surprise, causing them to rush to the hospital as fast as they could! Some of you arrived late, while others came weeks early. Every birth is an exciting event. Did you know that you just read the greatest birthday story of all? The Gospel writer Luke has just told you about the day Jesus was born. The Rescuer has been born! No more waiting! The day has arrived! The long chilly night of Israel's waiting is now over. Jesus is born.

REFLECTION AND INTERACTION

How do you think Mary felt when she realized that she was going to give birth to the Promised One?

Let's pray together to thank God for the birth of Jesus.

Memorize the big picture verse announcing good news of great joy: Luke 2:10-11.

> Q. How did the angel introduce Jesus as God's promised King?
>
> A. I bring you good news of a great joy that will be for all the people. For unto you is born this day in the city of David a Savior, who is Christ the Lord. (Luke 2:10–11)

Bible Reading: Luke 2:8–14; Genesis 12:1–3; Matthew 1:1–17 (esp. 1:1, 16–17)

Devotional Reading: Jesus Is the Savior for All People, from David's City, the Christ!

Can you imagine the excitement of the shepherds? They are working quietly on a dark night, watching sheep. Suddenly, an angel appears and brings the announcement: *A Savior has been born!* They will see the Savior with their own eyes. They will find him wrapped in clothes and lying in a manger. What an announcement! But there is more. The sky explodes with light and the praise of thousands of angels. The day has arrived. This is the moment. No more "a Savior is coming"—now the message is "the Savior has come!" The Rescuer is born. In this one announcement so many promises are fulfilled. First, the promise of "good news" or blessing for all peoples—God's promise to Abraham—is fulfilled. Second, God's promise concerning David's city is fulfilled. A Savior has been born in Bethlehem, King David's hometown. This is the town the prophet Micah said would be the birthplace of the promised ruler (Micah 5:2). Third, the promise of the Christ—or the King—is fulfilled. Jesus is God's anointed King. This one announcement by the angel fulfills all three of those promises. What an exciting day! What a message of joy—for all peoples! A Savior has been born in the town of David—just like God had promised!

REFLECTION AND INTERACTION

Why was the angel's message a message of great joy? What promises did the announcement fulfill?

Why is it important to read the New Testament in light of the Old?

> Q. **How did the angel introduce Jesus as God's promised King?**
>
> A. I bring you good news of a great joy that will be for all the people. For unto you is born this day in the city of David a Savior, who is Christ the Lord. (Luke 2:10–11)

Bible Reading: Luke 2:15–20

Devotional Reading: Responding to Jesus Like the Shepherds

Have you heard of *show-and-tell*? Can you explain what it is? Our Bible reading today has something like show-and-tell going on, only it's more like *see-and-tell*. When the angels went away, the shepherds were thrilled. They couldn't wait to see this baby! They rushed off to Bethlehem to find him. There they found him in a dirty stable with Mary and Joseph. Jesus was lying in a manger— a food trough for animals. The shepherd's hearts were filled with wonder. The angels had been right. Here was Christ the Lord. They could hardly stand it. They had seen the Rescuer! Having *seen* him they now just had to *tell* others. They hurried away from Bethlehem to tell other people. Everyone who heard the news was amazed. The shepherds kept on bursting with excitement. They couldn't stop praising God. They couldn't stop glorifying him. They couldn't stop telling others all that they had seen and heard!

REFLECTION AND INTERACTION

Doesn't reading the story of the shepherds finding Jesus make your heart burst with excitement? What would the game *read-and-tell* look like?

How can we be like the shepherds—praising God and telling others about this miracle? Who would you like to tell?

Why Jesus Came

Q. **How did John the Baptist introduce Jesus?**

A. Behold, the Lamb of God, who takes away the sin of the world! (John 1:29)

Bible Reading: John 1:29–34

Devotional Reading: The Witness of John the Baptist

Have you ever been so excited for others' arrival that you sat at the window, looking out for the first glimpse of them? What did you do as soon as you saw them? You probably shouted out for everyone to hear that the people you had been waiting for had arrived! John the Baptist was also on the lookout. He knew that a Rescuer was coming; God had told him. God had told John to watch for the One on whom the Holy Spirit would come down like a dove. When John saw the Spirit rest on Jesus, he had an announcement to make. He announced to everyone listening that Jesus was "the Lamb of God, who takes away the sin of the world." He announced who Jesus was, just like the angels at Jesus's birth. Jesus was the Lamb of God who would take away sins! What an exciting announcement!

REFLECTION AND INTERACTION

How did John the Baptist know that Jesus was the Rescuer?

What kind of Rescuer did John think Jesus would be? Do we need this kind of Rescuer?

Memorize this week's big picture verse: John 1:29.

> Q. How did John the Baptist introduce Jesus?
>
> A. Behold, the Lamb of God, who takes away the sin of the world! (John 1:29)

Bible Reading: John 1:29; Hebrews 9:1–28

Devotional Reading: Jesus's Death and Old Testament Sacrifices

Can you tell me something of the lesson about the Passover lamb? Do you remember anything about the sacrificial system Israel had in the Old Testament? We learned that without the shedding of blood, there is no forgiveness of sins. Remember how in the Old Testament the priests would kill a lamb for people's sins? Blood was a pointer. The priest would sprinkle God's altar with the lamb's blood. Thousands of lambs were killed for people's sins in the Old Testament. That is because God requires a very costly price for sin—death. In the Old Testament, year after year, priests would offer sacrifice after sacrifice, killing lamb after lamb, shedding blood and then more blood. Now, after recalling that, do you see the connection John the Baptist is making about Jesus and Old Testament sacrifices? Jesus, the Lamb of God, will die to take away the sins of the world. The sacrifice that Jesus will make, while similar to those of the Old Testament, is different—his sacrifice will be a one-time event! No more animals will need to die. Jesus's blood will be shed *once* to take away the sins of *many* people.

REFLECTION AND INTERACTION

Why does God require a life to be given in the place of the person who sins? What does the need for a sacrifice teach you about God's character?

Q. **How did John the Baptist introduce Jesus?**

A. Behold, the Lamb of God, who takes away the sin of the world! (John 1:29)

Bible Reading: John 1:29; 1 Peter 1:17–21

Devotional Reading: Redemption Obtained

The word *redeemed* is not one we hear often these days outside of church. Put simply, *redeemed* means "bought back." It's the idea that something you once owned has been taken, and to get it back you have to pay for it again. The Bible says that God redeemed us; God bought us back with the blood of Jesus. Our sins took us away from God, but Jesus exchanged, or traded, his life for ours when he died on the cross. In fact, the Bible reading today tells us that even before God made the world, he decided that Jesus, the Rescuer, would be a Lamb who would die. He would be a perfect Lamb, without any blemishes or defects. And when he bought us for himself, he bought us everlasting life.

REFLECTION AND INTERACTION

Why is the blood of Jesus precious to God?

How should we live if we know that we have been redeemed by Jesus's death?

Question 30

How Jesus Saves

Q. What did Jesus say would prove he was God's promised King?

A. Destroy this temple, and in three days I will raise it up. (John 2:19)

Bible Reading: John 2:13–22; 1 Kings 8:27–30

Devotional Reading: The Temple as the Place of God's Provision

If you draw a picture of a tree, is the tree you draw a real live tree? No, it's only a picture, isn't it? Suppose that I had never seen a tree, but you showed me your picture. Don't you think your picture would help me recognize a real tree when I finally did see one? Of course it would! Solomon's temple is a lot like a picture. It helps us recognize God's real Temple when we finally see it. Solomon's temple was where sacrifices for the forgiveness of sins were carried out. Whenever God's people saw the temple, they saw the picture of God forgiving their sins. When Jesus came, he came to replace the temple. He was not merely a picture of God forgiving sin; he was the perfect Temple, the final place of sacrifice for sin. That is why Jesus is greater than the temple. Today, we don't need a picture like the temple, because humankind has now seen the real Temple of God—Jesus.

REFLECTION AND INTERACTION

Where do we go to see God?

Where do we go to know that God still forgives sins?

Begin to memorize this week's big picture verse: John 2:19.

> **Q. What did Jesus say would prove he was God's promised King?**
>
> A. Destroy this temple, and in three days I will raise it up. (John 2:19)

Bible Reading: John 2:13–19

Devotional Reading: Jesus Cleansed the Temple

Do you know why Jesus was so angry at what was going on in the temple? The temple was built as a place to worship God. In other words, the temple was a place where God's people could go to meet with him, to pray to him, to praise him, to offer sacrifices to him, and to hear his Word. But by the time Jesus was born, the focus of the temple had changed. Now it was a hustling, bustling marketplace. Because of all the noise and clamoring crowds, many people were kept from truly worshiping God. That is why Jesus was so angry and drove out all of the people who were buying and selling animals in the temple. People had become more concerned about making money than they were about truly being sorry for breaking God's laws. By clearing the temple, Jesus was pointing out that the whole system of sacrifices in the temple was about to come to an end. Why? Because when Jesus offered himself on the cross for our sin, his sacrifice was so perfect, so powerful, and so pleasing to God that there was never any need for another sacrifice.

REFLECTION AND INTERACTION

What it would be like if you had to offer a sacrifice every time you sinned?

Why don't we need a temple or sacrifices anymore?

> Q. What did Jesus say would prove he was God's promised King?
>
> A. Destroy this temple, and in three days I will raise it up. (John 2:19)

Bible Reading: John 2:18–22; 20:30–31

Devotional Reading: Jesus Performed Signs "That You Might Believe"

What did today's Bible reading say the Jews demanded of Jesus after he cleared the temple? Verse 18 tells us the answer: "What sign do you show us?" They wanted a sign from Jesus. Let's list the different types of signs we might see in a day. We see stop signs, or signs on highways telling us where we are, or signs hanging in shop windows. But when the Gospel of John uses the word *sign*, it means something different. A sign in the Gospel of John is a special kind of miracle that Jesus did. It shows us who he is and what he came to do. Not only that, but Jesus did these signs so that people would believe in him and have eternal life. Jesus's signs were visible pictures to show Israel that he really was God's Son, the long-awaited king, who had come to establish God's kingdom. His greatest sign of all would be the destruction and resurrection of the Temple. Jesus would die and be raised to life again on the third day, just as he said.

REFLECTION AND INTERACTION

According to John, why did Jesus perform signs?

Does God need to do any more signs to prove to us that Jesus is his Son?

Question 31

You Must Be Born Again

Q. What must one do to see God's kingdom?

A. Unless one is born again he cannot see the kingdom of God. (John 3:3)

Bible Reading: John 3:1–3

Devotional Reading: Nicodemus Comes to See Jesus

If I were to ask you to tell me three things about yourself, what would you tell me? Today we are going to learn three things about the man who came to talk to Jesus at night. First, we learn that his name was Nicodemus, so we know that he was a Jewish man. Second, we learn where he went to school and what he did. John tells us that he was a Pharisee—that means he was well educated in a particular school that studied the Old Testament. We could call him a Bible expert. Third, we learn that he was a member of the ruling body over the Jewish people. He was an important leader and authority in Israel. John then tells us that Nicodemus thought he understood Jesus better than he actually did. At best, Nicodemus thought Jesus was a teacher, but not the Son of God. He also thought he could tell what Jesus was all about. But although Nicodemus was very smart and an expert in the Old Testament, he really didn't understand who Jesus was or what Jesus was doing. There are many people like Nicodemus today. They have decided that they know who Jesus is and what he came to do without even understanding the basics about Jesus and his teaching. The most basic thing is this: no one can see the kingdom of God unless he is born again.

REFLECTION AND INTERACTION

How can we avoid being like Nicodemus?

What are some misunderstandings people have about Jesus?

Memorize this week's big picture verse: John 3:3.

> **Q. What must one do to see God's kingdom?**
>
> A. Unless one is born again he cannot see the kingdom of God. (John 3:3)

Bible Reading: John 3:1–8

Devotional Reading: The Necessity of Being Born Again

Have you ever tried to describe a beautiful place you have seen to a friend who has never been there? It is very hard, isn't it? Sometimes the only way for others to really know what a beautiful place is like is to go there and see for themselves. Well, Jesus explains to Nicodemus that he cannot really understand what the kingdom of God is like unless he experiences it himself personally. Jesus calls this personal encounter with the kingdom being "born again." One has to be born again to see God's kingdom. Now, do you think that you can be born two times? That statement puzzled Nicodemus too. God's Spirit is the only one who can cause someone to be born again. Jesus explained that this encounter with the kingdom of God is a spiritual rebirth not a physical one. When he tells Nicodemus about "water, and the Spirit" and "the wind," he is trying to jog Nicodemus's memory of the Old Testament, which said we would be born again this way (see Ezekiel 36:25–37:10). Unfortunately, Nicodemus, the Old Testament expert, didn't make the connections that Jesus was trying to help him see. Nicodemus needed to learn the very basic truth that God was saving us from the inside out. And we need to learn that too.

REFLECTION AND INTERACTION

Can you list the three things needed to have a kingdom? Are you beginning to see that Jesus is *King*, we are his *people*, and our hearts are the *place* where his rule or kingdom is recognized?

How do you know if you are born again?

> Q. **What must one do to see God's kingdom?**
>
> A. Unless one is born again he cannot see the kingdom of God. (John 3:3)

Bible Reading: John 3:9–18

Devotional Reading: We Gain the Ability to Come to God through the Death of the Son of Man

Moses once made a snake out of bronze metal and put it on a pole (Numbers 21). Why did he do that? The Israelites had disobeyed God and rejected him as their King, so God punished them by sending snakes to bite them. If a snake bit someone, that person would die. But even though God was angry with his people, he still provided a way for them to survive the snakebite. God told Moses to make a bronze snake and hang it on a high pole near all the people. Whenever an Israelite who had been bitten by a snake looked at the bronze snake on the pole, that person would not die. In our Bible passage Nicodemus wasn't getting any of the clues Jesus was giving him about who he was. So Jesus ended the night's conversation by giving Nicodemus one last hint that might help him later: Jesus said that he would be like the snake that was lifted up on high. Everyone who trusts in his death on the cross will have eternal life.

REFLECTION AND INTERACTION

What does Nicodemus's response to Jesus tell us about what we might expect when we talk to people about who Jesus is and why he came?

How is Jesus like the snake on the pole?

Jesus Is the Resurrection

Q. How is one born again into God's kingdom?

A. Jesus said . . . , "I am the resurrection and the life. Whoever believes in me, though he die, yet shall he live." (John 11:25)

Bible Reading: John 11:1–6, 17–27

Devotional Reading: Jesus Has Power over Death

When we read the Bible, we get to listen in on what happened when Jesus spoke with people. I'm glad we get this chance, aren't you? Last week we listened in on a conversation between Jesus and Nicodemus, and we heard Jesus say that we must be born again. This week we find ourselves listening in on a conversation Jesus has with Martha after the death of her brother Lazarus. If we learned last week that we must be born again, we learn this week that Jesus has the power to do that for us. In fact, Jesus says that he is the resurrection. Wow! What a statement! Jesus has born-again power! After hearing things said about Jesus by the angels and John the Baptist, now we are hearing things said by Jesus that should give us great hope of being rescued from our bodies of sin.

REFLECTION AND INTERACTION

How does Jesus's statement about the resurrection help us with our fears?

This is a great week to learn our memory verse by singing the song "I Am the Resurrection and the Life" found on page 184.

> **Q. How is one born again into God's kingdom?**
>
> A. Jesus said . . . , "I am the resurrection and the life. Whoever believes in me, though he die, yet shall he live." (John 11:25)

Bible Reading: John 11:28–44

Devotional Reading: Jesus's Claim Must Be Backed Up with Action

Let's pretend that we are out on the school playground and I say to you, "I can throw this baseball over the school building." Let's also pretend that the building is twenty stories high. What might you say about my claim to throw the ball that far? I bet you might say something like, "Oh, really? I'll believe it when I see it." Or, "It is one thing to talk a big talk, but now you've got to prove it!" Sometimes talk doesn't mean anything without the actions to back it up. I couldn't really throw a ball over a twenty-story building. Do you think that some people may have wondered if Jesus's talk was cheap? Jesus claimed to be resurrection power, but saying it is one thing; proving it is another. How could Jesus prove such a statement? Right, he would have to raise Lazarus from the dead. And that is just what he did. By raising Lazarus from the dead, Jesus showed the people of his own day that he was the very person he claimed to be.

REFLECTION AND INTERACTION

Are you able to back up everything you say? How does this affect the way you view Jesus?

Take time to pray and thank Jesus for the power he has over death.

> **Q. How is one born again into God's kingdom?**
>
> A. Jesus said . . . , "I am the resurrection and the life. Whoever believes in me, though he die, yet shall he live." (John 11:25)

Bible Reading: John 11:1–16

Devotional Reading: Jesus Waited to Go to Lazarus to Show His Glory

Today we've gone back to the beginning of the Lazarus story. The story is about death, particularly the death of someone who was deeply loved by the people in the story. Death is a terrible thing. When someone dies, those who love that person are filled with deep sadness for a long time. Losing someone we love is perhaps the most difficult thing we will go through in this life. When we experience the death of someone we love, we may be tempted to ask God, "Why did he or she have to die?" Did you hear what Jesus said about why he allowed Lazarus to die in the first place? Lazarus's death was an opportunity to reveal the glory of God and his power over death. When you are faced with the death of someone you love, remember that God is at work in the world to show his glory. There will be a day when God's children will be raised out of death—Jesus has the power to raise the dead to newness of life. And that life will belong to all who put their faith in him.

REFLECTION AND INTERACTION

How can we prepare ourselves for death?

Sing the song "I Am the Resurrection and the Life" (p. 184) again to remember that Jesus has the power to give us what we really need—eternal life!

Jesus Is the Only Way

Q. Who is the only way to God?

A. Jesus said . . . , "I am the way, and the truth, and the life. No one comes to the Father except through me." (John 14:6)

Bible Reading: John 14:1–6

Devotional Reading: Jesus Says Another Amazing Thing

Over the last few weeks we've learned a lot about Jesus. We've learned about him by listening to what others said about him. During the first two weeks of our New Testament study, we heard what the angels and John the Baptist had to say about Jesus. He was the Promised One, the Savior, the King, the Lamb of God who would take away the sin of the world. For the past three weeks we have been learning about Jesus by listening to him talk: "Destroy this temple and in three days I will raise it up" (John 2:19). "Unless one is born again, he cannot see the kingdom of God" (3:3). "I am the resurrection and the life. Whoever believes in me, though he die, yet shall he live" (11:25). This week, we hear Jesus say, "I am the way, and the truth, and the life. No one comes to the Father except through me" (14:6). Don't miss what we are learning. The Gospel of John is helping us to know Jesus by telling us the *many promising words others said* about him, as well as by the *many words that he spoke* about himself.

REFLECTION AND INTERACTION

What do you think is the most amazing thing we've learned about Jesus in the last few weeks?

Sing the song "I Am the Way" found on page 185 to help you learn this week's big picture verse: John 14:6.

Brush up on the big picture verses you've learned.

> **Q. Who is the only way to God?**
>
> A. Jesus said . . . , "I am the way, and the truth, and the life. No one comes to the Father except through me." (John 14:6)

Bible Reading: John 14:1–9

Devotional Reading: Jesus Is the Way, and There Is No Other

What do you think the people around you—your neighbors and classmates perhaps—think about Jesus? Most people respect Jesus and his teachings. They love to quote him when he says things like, "Blessed are the poor . . . for theirs is the kingdom of heaven," and, "Blessed are those who mourn, for they will be comforted" (Matthew 6:3, 4). In general, most people think that Jesus said some wonderful things, and many believe the world would be a better place if we lived out his teachings. However, Jesus said some hard things too. Our memory verse for the week is a good example. The part that everyone likes is: "I am the way, and the truth, and the life." These words are no problem for people today. What they don't like is the second half of the verse: "No one comes to the Father except through me." That is tough for people to swallow! Jesus does not claim to be one of many ways to God. He says just the opposite—he is the only way to God. This is very important for you to know, because you live at a time when people reject this teaching of Jesus. People want to believe in Jesus and follow his teachings—but only those teachings that they agree with. The Bible, however, teaches that we must take Jesus at his word—all of it.

REFLECTION AND INTERACTION

There is a phrase that says, "You gotta take the good with the bad." Do you understand what it means? How does that relate to our big picture verse for this week?

Do the words "no one comes" cause you to pray for anyone? Why not pray for them now?

> **Q. Who is the only way to God?**
>
> A. Jesus said . . . , "I am the way, and the truth, and the life. No one comes to the Father except through me." (John 14:6)

Bible Reading: John 14:1–6

Devotional Reading: Jesus's Words Are Comforting

Jesus has been telling his disciples that he is going away. He has told them that he is going to die (John 12:20–33; 16:16), and they are sad. No wonder Thomas and Philip want to find out where Jesus is going and how they can get there. This is the moment, when the disciples are frightened and sad, that Jesus tells them not to worry. He says, "Let not your hearts be troubled. . . . I am the way." Some people get mad that Jesus says he is the only way to God; they want to find their own way. Do you think that the disciples were thinking, "Oh, what a bummer. It doesn't seem fair that there should be only one way to God." No way! How grateful the disciples must have been to be told that there is even one, single, solitary way back into a relationship with him.

REFLECTION AND INTERACTION

Why are these words of Jesus to his disciples comforting words?

Why is it important to know that there is only one way to God?

Jesus Is Crucified

> **Q. How was the way to God opened by Jesus?**
>
> A. They crucified him. (John 19:18)

Bible Reading: John 18:1–14

Devotional Reading: Jesus Is Arrested

Have you ever been playing a game when suddenly one of the players yells, "Hey, that's not fair!" What might make someone say that? When you heard our Bible reading for today, did something inside you make you want to yell, "Hey, that's not fair!" After all, did Jesus deserve to get arrested? Did he deserve to be betrayed by Judas? For weeks we have been reading things about Jesus. Can you remember anything he did that would make people want to arrest and kill him? Nevertheless, he was arrested. The Bible says, "So the band of soldiers and their captain and the officers of the Jews arrested Jesus." Listen now; we are coming to the most important part of our study. During the next two weeks we will see Jesus not only get arrested, but be tried in a court, beaten, and then crucified on the cross. Your reaction to Jesus's death can change how you live your life. Was his crucifixion fair or unfair? And if it was unfair, then what good could possibly come out of it?

REFLECTION AND INTERACTION

From all you have read about Jesus, do you think he deserved to be arrested? Why or why not?

In your own experience, does anything good ever come out of something unfair?

Memorize the big picture verse for this week: John 19:18.

> **Q. How was the way to God opened by Jesus?**
>
> A. They crucified him. (John 19:18)

Bible Reading: John 19:1–3, 13–16

Devotional Reading: Jesus Is Sentenced to Death on a Cross

The things that happen to people are not always fair—and sometimes things go from bad to worse. It is bad enough that Jesus was arrested, but to read that he was flogged, mocked, struck in the face, and then handed over to be crucified, well, that is much worse. I can't think of anything more unfair than this. Hopes for Jesus had been much higher than this disgraceful ending. The angels announced that he was going to be the Savior. John the Baptist told people that Jesus was going to take away the sin of the world. We were captivated by Jesus's own words about the kingdom, and the resurrection, and the Way. We saw his words backed up by his mighty work of raising Lazarus from the dead. But now, we find him sentenced to death on the cross. This really happened! This is not some made-up story. It happened. Jesus of Nazareth died a real death on a cross just outside of Jerusalem nearly two thousand years ago.

REFLECTION AND INTERACTION

What is so surprising about this part of the story of Jesus? How do you think Jesus's followers felt?

Do you find Jesus's death confusing? Do you think that any good could come out of it?

Q. How was the way to God opened by Jesus?

A. They crucified him. (John 19:18)

Bible Reading: John 18:38; 19:4–6, 12

Devotional Reading: Jesus Did Not Die for His Own Sins

What do you think John is trying to tell us in our Bible reading today? He wants us to know that Pilate thought Jesus was an innocent man. Pilate says, "I find no guilt in him" three different times. And Pilate tried to set Jesus free. Isn't that amazing? The judge who ordered Jesus to die never thought that he was guilty of any crime. Now, there are two important questions for you to think about. Are you ready? First, what is God's penalty for sin? Here's a hint: think about a command God gave Adam and Eve in the garden of Eden. The answer is *death*. God told Adam and Eve that if they disobeyed his word they would "surely die" (Genesis 2:17). Second, if Jesus never sinned, and even Pilate thought that he was innocent, then could Jesus have possibly been paying the penalty for his own sins? No, of course not. This presents us with a mystery we will explain next week. If Jesus didn't die for any sins that he committed, then why did God allow him to die at all?

REFLECTION AND INTERACTION

Why do you think Pilate decided to crucify Jesus, even when he thought he was innocent? (Hint: John 19:12–13.) What does that tell you about Pilate?

Why is it important to understand that Jesus wasn't crucified for his own sins?

Jesus Died for Our Sins

> **Q. Did Jesus say God's promise was fulfilled when he was crucified?**
>
> **A.** [Jesus] said, "It is finished." (John 19:30)

Bible Reading: John 19:16–18, 28–30

Devotional Reading: Jesus Was Victorious on the Cross

Do you know what a mystery is? A mystery is something that can't be understood, unless someone explains it to you. Remember when we wondered how God could allow Jesus to die on the cross if he had never committed any sins? This week we will unravel that mystery. Jesus wasn't dying for sins that he had committed; rather, he was dying for *our* sins. His death was fulfilling God's rescue plan. And so, when Jesus had done everything God had asked him to do on the earth, he called out in a loud voice, "It is finished!" Jesus said these words like someone who just finished doing something great. He accomplished his goal. He finished his task. He was the perfect sacrifice for sins. If you want to know if your sins are forgiven, look back to the death of Jesus. He is the only perfect sacrifice for our sin. And his death is the answer to the mystery of how God would rescue us from sin. God sent his only Son to pay the penalty for our disobedience.

REFLECTION AND INTERACTION

How do you think Jesus felt about finishing the work of paying for our sin?

What does Jesus's death on the cross teach you about God's love for you?

Memorize this week's big picture verse: John 19:30.

> **Q. Did Jesus say God's promise was fulfilled when he was crucified?**
>
> A. [Jesus] said, "It is finished." (John 19:30)

Bible Reading: Genesis 3:23; 6:17; Exodus 12:21; Isaiah 5:13; John 2:19

Devotional Reading: God Banished Jesus from His Presence for Us

We read five different verses from the Bible today—and they were all memory verses from earlier times in our devotional. Each one points us to being able to understand what was happening when Jesus died on the cross. Jesus was banished for our sins. Jesus perished. Jesus was the sacrificial Lamb. Jesus represents God's people who go into exile. Jesus's death is the destruction of the Temple. The Bible has been showing us all along the penalty for sin. It requires separation from God. He banished Adam and Eve from the garden; he caused everything to perish in the flood; he killed all the firstborn Egyptians at the time of the Exodus; he sent Israel into exile; and he had Solomon's temple destroyed to show that he was separated from his people because of their sin. Now, Jesus's death shows us what all those events meant. Jesus takes on the punishment for the sin of his people. He was abandoned by God when he died on the cross (Mark 15:33–34). In his death you see the extent of God's love for you!

REFLECTION AND INTERACTION

Do you see how the New Testament helps us understand the Old Testament?

Thank God for giving us all the clues we need to understand the mystery of his great love.

Q. Did Jesus say God's promise was fulfilled when he was crucified?

A. [Jesus] said, "It is finished." (John 19:30)

Bible Reading: John 19:30

Devotional Reading: Jesus's Death Is the
Good News of God's Rescue

Let's do a quick review of the Gospel of John. First, we heard things *said about Jesus*. Do you remember the words of the angels and John the Baptist? Then we listened to the many things *Jesus said and did*. Remember his words about the temple, the kingdom, the resurrection, and the Way? We even learned that Jesus raised someone from the dead. Next we saw what *others did to Jesus*. They crucified him on the cross. And this week we are learning about what *Jesus said about what they did*: "It is finished!" The Gospel of John gives us the words and actions of others and the words and actions of Jesus to help us see that Jesus's death is God's plan to rescue us from sin.

REFLECTION AND INTERACTION

Do you believe that Jesus died on the cross to rescue you from your sin?

If actions speak louder than words, what does Jesus's death on the cross mean to you?

Jesus Rose from the Dead

> Q. How did Thomas respond to Jesus after the resurrection?
>
> A. Thomas answered him, "My Lord and my God!" (John 20:28)

Bible Reading: John 20:1–8, 19–20, 24–29

Devotional Reading: The Surprise of Easter

Have you ever been so surprised by seeing someone that the shock made you gasp for air? Just such a surprise happened to the followers of Jesus, especially Thomas. The two days after Jesus's crucifixion had been the most difficult days his friends could remember. Jesus, the one they had hoped was the Messiah, had been crucified, was dead, and buried. His followers were all very sad. They never imagined that this was how it would all end. But the third day had now come, and they were beginning to deal with the reality that Jesus was no longer with them. On that morning some of Jesus's friends went to the tomb. When they got there, the tomb was open and Jesus's body was not there. They wondered what was going on. Had someone taken the body away? Their sadness turned to confusion, but later, they saw him alive and were shocked! He had risen from the dead! Finally Thomas saw him too. What an exciting day that first Easter must have been.

REFLECTION AND INTERACTION

How surprised do you think the disciples were to learn that Jesus was alive?

Sing the song "My Lord, My God" found on pages 186–87.

Begin to memorize this week's verse: John 20:28.

> Q. How did Thomas respond to Jesus after the resurrection?
>
> A. Thomas answered him, "My Lord and my God!" (John 20:28)

Bible Reading: John 20:24–30

Devotional Reading: The Necessity of Easter

Today there are two questions to answer. First, do you have any idea how Jesus could rise from the dead? The answer is something we learned earlier. Jesus is the resurrection and the life—the way, the truth, and the life. Since Jesus is life itself, Jesus could not stay dead. And since Jesus had never sinned, he did not deserve the punishment for sin—and death could not rightly hold him. His resurrection was bound to happen. Second, what do Thomas's words, "My Lord and my God," teach you about Jesus? Part of the answer is simple; they teach us that Jesus is, in fact, the Son of God. He is God in the flesh. But the words of Thomas also teach us that Jesus is Lord. And the word *Lord* means master, one who has human authority. The resurrection of Jesus doesn't prove to us only that he is God, but it teaches us that he is the perfect man too! It tells us that Jesus never did anything wrong. Since death is the penalty for every man or woman who sins, then Jesus's resurrection from the dead must be the reward for living perfectly. No wonder Thomas put it like he did: "My Lord and my God!" In all his humanity, Jesus is the one and only person who can rightfully stand, on his own merit, in the presence of God. That gives us great hope of standing there too!

REFLECTION AND INTERACTION

Can you say in your own words why the resurrection of Jesus is so important?

What does the resurrection of Jesus prove to you about Jesus?

Q. How did Thomas respond to Jesus after the resurrection?

A. Thomas answered him, "My Lord and my God!" (John 20:28)

Bible Reading: Genesis 12:1–3; 2 Samuel 7:12; 2 Chronicles 6:2; Jeremiah 29:14; John 2:19

Devotional Reading: The Triumph of Easter

What are some things that might help you on a treasure hunt? You certainly would need a map or clues along the way, wouldn't you? Our devotionals have been leading us on a treasure hunt. Our Bible readings for today were past clues that help us know that we have found our greatest treasure in Jesus. In fact, his resurrection from the dead explains all the clues we have been picking up. His resurrection is the temple rebuilt—the Old Testament time of rebuilding the temple was the clue. He is the returning person from exile—the Old Testament returning people were the clues. His resurrection is proof that he is the King of kings who will reign forever—King David is the clue. And his resurrection is the fulfillment of God's promise to bless all the families of the earth—the promise to Abraham was the clue. In Jesus's resurrection we find God's greatest treasure!

REFLECTION AND INTERACTION

How does the resurrection help you to praise God?

Praise God for his surprising, necessary, and triumphant plan for salvation in song and in prayer.

Jesus Fulfills God's Promise

Review 1: Reviewing the Gospel of John

Do you see how the Gospel of John is put together? The emphasis in the first half is on the teachings and signs (miracles) of Jesus. The second half, from chapter 13 on, is devoted entirely to the death and resurrection of Jesus. The latter half covers only the last days of Jesus life. The point John is making is clear: if you want to know what Jesus's life was about, you must read about his death and resurrection. We divided up the Gospel like this:

> The Promising Words of Others about Jesus (Questions 28 and 29)
> The Provocative Words and Actions of Jesus (Questions 30 to 33)
> The Problematic Death of Jesus (Question 34)
> The Provocative Words of Jesus in Death (Question 35)
> The Promising Words of Others at the Resurrection of Jesus
>   (Question 36)

Review 2: Reviewing the Death and Resurrection of Jesus

One of the important things to reinforce during this week of review are the connections between the gospel and what we learned in the Old Testament. Here is one of them: Jesus's death is the fulfillment of all the Old Testament teaching on the penalty for sin. The Old Testament tells us that Adam and Eve were banished; the world perished at the time of the flood; a sacrificial lamb was required; the people were sent away into exile; and the temple was destroyed. In all these ways, the Old Testament has been laying the foundation for us to make sense of Jesus's death. His death on the cross interprets all these events. He has become Israel under judgment. His death was substitutionary. He took our banishment, our perishing, our sacrifice, and our exile from God. Talk about these connections with your children this week.

Review 3: Reviewing the Importance of the Resurrection

The apostle Paul tells us that our faith in Christ is in vain if the resurrection did not really happen. It is that important! Talk with your kids this week about the resurrection of Jesus. Just as his death is prefigured in the Old Testament, so too is his resurrection. Remember Jesus's words: "Destroy this temple, and in three days I will raise it up" (John 2:19)? Jesus was speaking of his body, which would be raised on the third day. The connections to the Old Testament sections about the rebuilding of the temple should not be lost on you or your children. The Old Testament tells of the rebuilding of the temple; Jesus's own temple was restored on the third day. The Old Testament tells of the reentry of Israel into the land; Jesus's resurrection paves the way for his own reentry into heaven, the place of dwelling with God.

Remember, *The Big Picture Family Devotional* gives you a chance to work on all three areas of the trivium with your children. The grammar of the devotional is found in the big picture verses. Logic is understanding how each verse relates to another to create a coherent storyline. And the review weeks are the time for rhetoric. They allow you to test yourselves in your ability to restate what these weeks have been about. Be encouraged. You are teaching your children how to think by using this devotional!

Keep working this week on memorizing the big picture verses and tracing the storyline.

PART 5

God Completes His Promise

Questions 37–45

Spreading the Gospel of Jesus

Q. How did Jesus say word of his victory would spread?

A. You will receive power when the Holy Spirit has come upon you, and you will be my witnesses in Jerusalem and in all Judea and Samaria, and to the end of the earth. (Acts 1:8)

Bible Reading: Acts 1:1–11

Devotional Reading: Jesus's Charge to the Apostles

Imagine that there is a large box just in front of where you are sitting. Can you see it? Now, pretend that when we open it, we find a slightly smaller box. When we open that one, we find yet another smaller box. Imagine that this goes on and on until we are left with the tiniest of boxes with a present inside. Wouldn't we be amazed to be given a surprise box like that? Well, the Bible is like that box. We find surprise after surprise inside: the surprise that God created us and loves us; the surprise of Jesus's death and resurrection; and today, the surprise of Jesus's ascension back into heaven. King Jesus didn't stay on earth to begin his kingdom; he went back into heaven. He sent the Holy Spirit and decided to use people to spread the news of his victory! Jesus's return to heaven proves that there is one man who can rightly live with God. Back he went into the garden of God's presence! Back to the Promised Land, the place where God lives. Jesus's ascension into heaven is another one of God's surprises. What it must have been like to see that! What a surprise to learn that you were chosen to spread the message of his victory to the ends of the earth!

REFLECTION AND INTERACTION

Why is the ascension of Jesus a comforting thing for us?

What was the charge Jesus gave the apostles, and what tool did he give to help them with their task?

Memorize the big picture verse for this week: Acts 1:8.

> **Q. How did Jesus say word of his victory would spread?**
>
> **A.** You will receive power when the Holy Spirit has come upon you, and you will be my witnesses in Jerusalem and in all Judea and Samaria, and to the end of the earth. (Acts 1:8)

Bible Reading: Acts 2:38–41; 6:7; 8:25; 11:19–21; 28:30–31

Devotional Reading: The Apostles Spread the Message of Jesus's Victory

Planting a tree on Arbor Day can be fun. After choosing a good spot and digging a hole, you place the young sapling into the ground and tuck the moist soil back in around the roots. With the right amount of sun and water, your tree will grow. It will grow and grow and grow even as you grow! Imagine coming back to visit your tree twenty or thirty years after planting it. Do you have any idea how big it would be? Some trees grow to be dozens and dozens of feet high. When the disciples of Jesus shared the gospel message with the people of their day, it grew and grew and grew! First, it grew in Jerusalem. Acts 6:7 tells us that here even some of the priests became followers of Jesus. Then, the gospel message spread to Judea and Samaria, as Stephen and Philip shared the story with those who were half-Jewish, the Samaritans. Then Cornelius believed (Acts 10:1–33). He was the first non-Jewish believer. Finally, as the book of Acts closes, we find Paul sharing the gospel in the city of Rome—which at that time was the ends of the earth! The spread of the good news all happened just as Jesus had said it would. People who follow Jesus have the joy of bringing the gospel to the ends of the earth.

REFLECTION AND INTERACTION

How is the spread of the gospel in the book of Acts like a tree that just keeps on growing?

How could you help spread the gospel message? Is there anyone that you want to tell about Jesus? Pray for a chance today!

> Q. How did Jesus say word of his victory would spread?
>
> A. You will receive power when the Holy Spirit has come upon you, and you will be my witnesses in Jerusalem and in all Judea and Samaria, and to the end of the earth. (Acts 1:8)

Bible Reading: 1 Corinthians 15:1–8; 1 John 1:1–4

Devotional Reading: Witnesses Are Important

Suppose someone told you that he had a spaceship, one that could really go to the moon and back. Would you believe him? Would you be more or less likely to believe him if he wouldn't let you see it? Why? It is very hard to believe in something that you can't see, isn't it? In the same way, it would be very hard to believe that Jesus rose from the dead if there had been no witnesses. God knows that it is hard to believe without witnesses; that is why the apostles are so important. The Bible tells us that more than five hundred people saw Jesus after the resurrection. And John, the disciple, tells us that he touched him and saw him too! If you lived two thousands years ago in Palestine, you might have seen Jesus after the resurrection. But, you and I live at a different time. For us, believing in the witness of the people back then is what is important. Jesus is risen. You can trust the witnesses.

REFLECTION AND INTERACTION

Why is it important that people saw Jesus after the resurrection?

Take some time to catch up on your big picture verses.

Question 38

Peter Defines the Gospel

Q. What message did Peter spread?

A. [Jesus] is the one appointed by God to be judge of the living and the dead. To him all the prophets bear witness that everyone who believes in him receives forgiveness of sins through his name. (Acts 10:42–43)

Bible Reading: Acts 10:34–43; Hebrews 10:26–31

Devotional Reading: Jesus Is the Judge of the Living and the Dead

Sometimes we give great people a title that describes their greatness. For instance, basketball player Michael Jordan has the title "Six-Time World Champion." Gymnast Gabby Douglas earned the title "Olympic Gold Medalist." In England, Elizabeth gets the title "Queen." And in our Bible reading today, God gives to Jesus the title of "Judge." Jesus's resurrection from the dead is what gave him this great title. He is the only man who is great enough to judge everyone, because he never did anything wrong. In fact, his death paid for our wrongdoing. So God has made Jesus our Judge. Do you know what a judge does? A judge determines who is guilty of crimes and who is innocent. A judge punishes the guilty and sets the innocent free. That is what Jesus will do. If we don't ask him to forgive our sins, then he will punish us. But, if we trust his death as payment for our sin, then he will call us innocent. Jesus is our Judge. His resurrection means that we are all subject to him.

REFLECTION AND INTERACTION

What is God teaching us by giving Jesus the title of *Judge*?

Learn the song "No Favorites" found on pages 188–89.

Begin to memorize this week's verse: Acts 10:42–43.

> **Q. What message did Peter spread?**
>
> A. [Jesus] is the one appointed by God to be judge of the living and the dead. To him all the prophets bear witness that everyone who believes in him receives forgiveness of sins through his name. (Acts 10:42–43)

Bible Reading: Acts 10:42–43

Devotional Reading: There Is One Bible and One True God

Think about the stories you know from the Old Testament. There we find a lot of battle stories as well as stories of Israel's failures and God's judgment. What about the New Testament? It contains stories about Jesus healing people and forgiving their sins. Most people think that the Old Testament presents us with a God who is Judge. It isn't until the New Testament, so they say, that God appears to be loving and forgiving. But our verses say the opposite! On the basis of the resurrection of Jesus in the New Testament, Jesus is called "Judge." On the testimony of the prophets in the Old Testament, we learn that God is forgiving. Isn't that the opposite of what we might expect? We learn about a loving God who forgives sins in the Old Testament, and about the one whom God appointed as Judge in the New Testament!

REFLECTION AND INTERACTION

Give some examples from the Old Testament that show us that God forgives.

Since Jesus has already been appointed as our Judge, how should we live?

> **Q. What message did Peter spread?**
>
> A. [Jesus] is the one appointed by God to be judge of the living and the dead. To him all the prophets bear witness that everyone who believes in him receives forgiveness of sins through his name. (Acts 10:42–43)

Bible Reading: Acts 2:36–40

Devotional Reading: Forgiveness from Sins Comes through Jesus's Death and Resurrection

One day the apostle Peter was teaching a huge crowd about Jesus. After he explained to them that they were sinners and would be punished by God, they asked him if there was any escape from their problem. They asked him the biggest question of all: "What shall we do?" When the people asked Peter what they should do, he needed to have the right answer. Fortunately, he did. He told them,: "Repent and be baptized every one of you in the name of Jesus Christ for the forgiveness of your sins." They had to turn from their sins, ask Jesus for forgiveness, and be baptized in his name. Did you notice the only name in Peter's answer? The name of Jesus Christ! You see, it is only through his death and resurrection that we can be saved. It is only in Jesus's name that we can be rescued. Praise God that he gives us the right answer and a way out of our problem.

REFLECTION AND INTERACTION

Some people think God gave many ways to be rescued, but what does the Bible teach?

Thank God for sending Jesus and making a way for us to be rescued from sin.

Paul Defines the Gospel

> **Q. What message did Paul spread?**
>
> **A.** [Jesus] was delivered up for our trespasses and raised for our justification. (Romans 4:25)

Bible Reading: Romans 4:25

Devotional Reading: Jesus's Death Was for Our Sins

Do you like trains? There are all kinds of trains—locomotives, steam engines, freight, even toy electric trains that can speed along a track in your own home. But although there are many kinds of trains, they all have one thing in common. They all run on train tracks; and they run not on one track but two—two rails that run parallel to one another. Both rails are necessary. Without two tracks, trains couldn't go anywhere. Our memory verse this week is like a train track. Did you notice the two parallel parts? The first track says that Jesus died for our sins. That is plain enough. The second part, though, is just as important for our salvation. He was raised to life for our justification. Jesus's death is for our sins, and his resurrection is for our justification. We need his death and we also need his resurrection. Tomorrow we will learn what *justification* means.

REFLECTION AND INTERACTION

What does the death of Jesus teach us about God?

What does the resurrection teach us about God's love?

Begin to memorize this week's verse: Romans 4:25.

Q. **What message did Paul spread?**

A. [Jesus] was delivered up for our trespasses and raised for our justification. (Romans 4:25)

Bible Reading: Romans 4:1–8, 25

Devotional Reading: Jesus's Resurrection Was for Our Justification

Have you ever seen a courtroom? Perhaps you've seen one on television. The judge is the most important person in the courtroom. The judge has to know all the laws and be able to sort out who is right and who is wrong. Sometimes the judge's job isn't easy. If you had ever been accused of doing something wrong and had to go before a judge, he or she would listen to all the evidence and then make a decision on your case. The Bible verse for this week says that we are *justified* by Jesus's resurrection. That means that although our sins make us guilty before God, he declares us righteous—without any sin—because Jesus already paid for them. Jesus's resurrection is proof of that fact. Wow. The gospel contains the good news of knowing that when you or I stand before God, we can be justified because of Jesus. We don't work for eternal life. We don't deserve life. But we receive it in Jesus who was raised to life for our justification.

REFLECTION AND INTERACTION

What does it mean that God declared us righteous? How does that make you feel?

Memorize this week's important big picture verse: Romans 4:25.

> **Q. What message did Paul spread?**
>
> **A.** [Jesus] was delivered up for our trespasses and raised for our justification. (Romans 4:25)

Bible Reading: Romans 4:1–5

Devotional Reading: The Gospel Is for Us Who Are Corrupted

When we get to heaven, do you think that there will be any people there who did some really bad things while they lived on earth? The answer might surprise you. There will be. That is because the gospel is for corrupt and ungodly people! Did you see the way our Bible reading put it today? It said, "To the one who does not work but belives in him *who justifies the ungodly*, his faith is counted as righteousness." That means that we are made right before God by trusting in Jesus, not by doing good things or avoiding doing bad things. We all sin and are ungodly in God's sight. Even one sin that we might not think is such a bad thing, like lying to our parents or wishing we had someone else's toys, makes us ungodly. So, isn't the gospel great news for everyone? It is so strong that it can justify corrupt people—*people like you and me*! So many people try to get to heaven by doing good things, and so many others don't even try because they think they are too bad. But the good news is that God justifies the ungodly, not by works, but because of faith in Jesus. Isn't that the greatest truth you could imagine? No one is beyond God's grace.

REFLECTION AND INTERACTION

Do only good people get to heaven?

Can anyone earn his or her way into heaven? What must we do?

Believing the Gospel

Q. How do we obey God's word?

A. For by grace you have been saved through faith. And this is not your own doing; it is the gift of God, not a result of works, so that no one may boast. (Ephesians 2:8–9)

Bible Reading: Ephesians 2:1–10

Devotional Reading: Faith Is a Gift of God

Can a dead person play soccer? Can a dead person play tag? Can a dead person do anything at all? No, of course not. So, then, can a spiritually dead person— a person that is sinful and therefore separated from God—do anything at all to get rescued from sin? No. Only God has the power to make a spiritually dead person come alive. Only God can save us from our sins. The Bible verse for this week says that we are saved when God gives us faith. It teaches us that faith is not from ourselves; rather, it is a gift from God. Can you think of a better gift? God is so gracious to us that he not only sent his Son to die for us, but he sent his Holy Spirit to give us faith to believe in him. Faith is a wonderful present from God.

REFLECTION AND INTERACTION

What does the fact that faith itself is a gift from God teach you about God?

Sing the song "Saved by Grace" found on page 190.

Memorize this week's big picture verse: Ephesians 2:8–9.

> **Q. How do we obey God's word?**
>
> A. For by grace you have been saved through faith. And this is not your own doing; it is the gift of God, not a result of works, so that no one may boast. (Ephesians 2:8–9)

Bible Reading: Romans 3:21–31; 5:1–2

Devotional Reading: Justified before God

If we have learned anything from reading through the Bible, we know that people are unable to keep God's law. We may try very hard, but we all fall short. We stand guilty before a holy and righteous God. Thankfully, we have also learned that God rescued us through the death and resurrection of his Son, Jesus. Jesus was not like us. He kept the law. He was holy and righteous. When he stands before God, he is completely innocent. Not only that, but we learned that he took on our sins in his death. He was our substitute. He is the only way we can ever stand before God and be declared justified. To be declared justified before God is a huge thing! It is just as if I'd never sinned and just as if I'd kept the law. It means that God calls you a righteous person. Now you can live with him forever. Some people think that we are justified by doing good things and by obeying God's law, but that view is wrong. None of us can keep the law. We are justified through faith in Christ alone.

REFLECTION AND INTERACTION

Why is it important to be justified before God?

Why is it so important to ask God to give us faith in Jesus?

Q. **How do we obey God's word?**

A. For by grace you have been saved through faith. And this is not your own doing; it is the gift of God, not a result of works, so that no one may boast. (Ephesians 2:8–9)

Bible Reading: John 3:16; Hebrews 10:19–23

Devotional Reading: Faith Is Responding to God

This week we have learned that faith is a gift from God. It is because of faith in Christ, alone, that God declares us justified. We have learned the importance of asking God for faith. Do you find yourself asking God for faith? If so, that's good! The Bible teaches us that someone who is eager for faith has to do two things. First, you are to *repent*. To repent means to completely change your way of thinking about yourself and God. You must turn your mind from sinful things. You must stop thinking you are a king (or a queen) and can do whatever you want. You must declare that Jesus alone is King over all things, including you. You must now obey him. Second, you must *believe*. You must believe that Jesus came to die for sinners just like you. You must believe that Jesus's resurrection proves him to be God's Son. You can respond to God's great rescue plan by repenting from sin and believing in Jesus.

REFLECTION AND INTERACTION

What does *repentance* mean? What do you need to repent from?

In whom must we believe?

Question 41

Living as People Set Apart

> **Q. What kind of life is God calling us to live?**
>
> A. God has not called us for impurity, but in holiness.
> (1 Thessalonians 4:7)

Bible Reading: 1 Thessalonians 4:1–8; Galatians 5:16–25

Devotional Reading: By the Power of the Holy
Spirit We Are Saved from Sin to Holiness

What is the most powerful thing you can think of? Why would you say it is powerful? It probably causes things to move or change whether they want to or not. Think of a powerful tornado throwing around trucks and houses! Or think of an elephant moving a tree out of the way. Sin is also a very powerful thing. It is ugly and dark and stronger than any one of us. The Bible teaches us that sin was stronger than Adam and Eve. They couldn't stop sinning once they began. We know that sin was stronger than the people of Noah's day. Sin was even stronger than the people of Israel after they received God's law. But sin wasn't stronger than Jesus! He was stronger than sin. And by the power of his Spirit in us we too can begin to obey God. When we talk about leaving sin and obeying God, we use a big word: *sanctification*. To be *sanctified* means to be set apart for God to be holy. God saved us to be holy. And the power of the Holy Spirit, which is stronger than sin, enables us to overcome sin and live a holy life.

REFLECTION AND INTERACTION

How are we sanctified?

What does the fact that God is sanctifying us teach us about God's love?

List areas in your life that you need the Holy Spirit to change. Pray about them.

Begin to memorize this week's big picture verse: 1 Thessalonians 4:7.

Q. **What kind of life is God calling us to live?**

A. God has not called us for impurity, but in holiness.
    (1 Thessalonians 4:7)

Bible Reading: Romans 6:1–14

Devotional Reading: We Are Dead to Sin and Alive to God

Name some things that are opposites. Would you call life and death opposites? Certainly. Those who believe in Jesus have moved from one opposite to another. They have moved from death into life. Since a Christian is now spiritually alive, they should no longer act as they did when they were spiritually dead. People who are spiritually dead are slaves to sin—they do sinful things all the time. They are always disobeying God. People who are spiritually alive are slaves to God! They now serve him instead of sin. In living a Christian life, you will find yourself seeking to please God and obey him. Live for God now! You are dead to sin.

REFLECTION AND INTERACTION

What does a spiritually alive person look like?

How would you know if you had moved from death into life?

Q. **What kind of life is God calling us to live?**

A. God has not called us for impurity, but in holiness.
(1 Thessalonians 4:7)

Bible Reading: Hebrews 10:19–25

Devotional Reading: The Importance of the Church for Growth

What does the word *church* mean? The Bible identifies a "church" as believers, the people of God. However, the word *church* is commonly used in sentences like, "That's a nice steeple on that church." Or, "Hurry up everyone. We don't want to be late for church!" The church is the people of God, not the buildings where they meet. Because God now lives in us through his Spirit, the Bible calls us his "house." As members of his church, we have a special love for his people. We ought to meet regularly together to strengthen that love. Being with God's people is very important for us to grow in our faith. When the Bible is taught, God's voice is heard. As we hear from God, we know how to live. As we live in obedience to him, others will come to know him too.

REFLECTION AND INTERACTION

What is the church of Jesus Christ?

Why is meeting together as God's family important your growth as a Christian?

Living as God's New Creation

Q. How do we know if we are in Christ?

A. We have come to share in Christ, if indeed we hold our original confidence firm to the end. (Hebrews 3:14)

Bible Reading: Hebrews 3:12–4:5

Devotional Reading: Hold on to Your Faith

If you were running in a race, would you rather start well but not finish, or finish but not start well? Is it better to be quick at the beginning and then stop, or to start slow and finish the race in the end? It is better to finish, isn't it? One Olympic runner finished a marathon more than an hour after the first runner had already crossed the finish line. Afterward, people asked him why he didn't just quit. What is the point of finishing the race if you are more than an hour behind the leader? He responded that his country did not send him all the way to the Olympics to start a race; they sent him to finish it. That story illustrates what our text is saying about our own race of faith. We must finish! Don't stop believing! Hold on firmly till the end.

REFLECTION AND INTERACTION

How are we told to exercise our faith throughout life?

What does it mean to hold on firmly till the end?

Begin to memorize this week's big picture verse: Hebrews 3:14

> **Q. How do we know if we are in Christ?**
>
> **A.** We have come to share in Christ, if indeed we hold our original confidence firm to the end. (Hebrews 3:14)

Bible Reading: 2 Corinthians 5:17; John 15:4–11

Devotional Reading: We Are "in Christ"

Have you ever seen a branch that has fallen off a tree? Because that branch is no longer connected, it will die and rot away, won't it? It will die because it can't live without the life it received from the tree. Jesus uses a similar example to explain how important he is when it comes to our ability to know God. He said that we are all like branches, and that he is the vine. If we want to live, we must remain attached to him. In other words, we must be "in Christ." That same phrase is in our verse for this week: "We have come to share in Christ, if indeed we hold our original confidence firm to the end." If we are to be part of the new creation of God, we must never go back to attaching ourselves to the old ways of trying to know God. Rather, we must remain attached to the true way of knowing God, by grace through faith in Jesus.

REFLECTION AND INTERACTION

What are we learning about how we are to remain "in Christ"?

Who gives us life? Who enables us to be rescued and made part of the new creation?

> **Q. How do we know if we are in Christ?**
>
> A. We have come to share in Christ, if indeed we hold our original confidence firm to the end. (Hebrews 3:14)

Bible Reading: 2 Corinthians 5:17; Romans 8:10–17

Devotional Reading: You Are a "New Creature"

Do you think most people would rather have a new clean car or an old rusty one? How about socks? New ones, or old smelly ones with holes in them? The Bible says that "if anyone is in Christ, he is a new creation." Did you hear that? A new creation. Think of that! Everything that we were, because of Adam's sin, has been reversed in Jesus's death and resurrection. There is no more power of rusty old sin—no more smelly sin that holds us. Jesus is God's King over a new and rescued creation. Gone are the days of being servants to sin. Christ is making all things new. It is like returning to the garden of Eden and seeing the effects of sin being reversed. Jesus is restoring people to God. Jesus can make people follow God from the bottom of their hearts.

REFLECTION AND INTERACTION

How great would it be to be made new, with a desire to follow God's words?

Who is it that has the power to make someone a "new creation"?

Question 43

Living as People with Hope

Q. What promise will complete the rescue of God's people?

A. We are waiting for new heavens and a new earth in which righteousness dwells. (2 Peter 3:13)

Bible Reading: 2 Peter 3:3–13

Devotional Reading: God's Rescue Plan Will Come to Complete Fulfillment

Think of how you feel when your birthday is coming. The closer it gets, the harder it is to wait. You wish it would just hurry up and be your birthday so that you could celebrate. Most importantly, you can't wait to get your presents! Waiting for the end of God's rescue plan is a little bit like this. It ought to fill us with joyful anticipation. We read in the Bible that Jesus is coming again. Nobody knows when Jesus is coming again, but we do know that when he comes, everything on this earth will be destroyed. Should we be afraid of this? No. We look forward to Jesus's coming because when he comes again there will be a new heaven and a new earth, free from all the sin and sadness in this life. The Bible tells us of a special place where all of God's people will live with him forever. That will be a very wonderful day indeed—better than any birthday.

REFLECTION AND INTERACTION

What does the return of Jesus tell us about how God feels about the way things are in this world?

When you think about Jesus's return, how does that make you want to live?

Begin to memorize this week's verse: 2 Peter 3:13.

> Q. What promise will complete the rescue of God's people?
>
> A. We are waiting for new heavens and a new earth in which righteousness dwells. (2 Peter 3:13)

Bible Reading: Genesis 1:1; 2 Peter 3:13; Revelation 21:1–7

Devotional Reading: The Bible Ends as It Begins

Do you remember the answer to the question, "Who created the heavens and the earth?" It is: "In the beginning, God created the heavens and the earth." Do you ever wonder what God is going to do after this present earth is destroyed by fire? We learned in our Bible reading that we should be looking forward to a new heaven and a new earth. This new place will be more wonderful than anything you could ever imagine. The new heaven and the new earth will be a place where God's children live with God. There will be no crying, no pain, and no sadness. God will be our God and we will be his people. We will live together forever in perfect happiness and peace. The perfect relationship that God had with Adam and Eve before the fall will be completely restored! Heaven will be that good.

REFLECTION AND INTERACTION

What do you think the new heaven and new earth will be like?

What does God's plan for an eternal heaven tell you about his love for us?

> **Q. What promise will complete the rescue of God's people?**
>
> **A.** We are waiting for new heavens and a new earth in which righteousness dwells. (2 Peter 3:13)

Bible Reading: 2 Peter 3:11–18

Devotional Reading: The Hope of Heaven
Motivates Our Present Behavior

Have you ever heard people say, "Well, I guess we will just have to kill some time"? What do you think they mean by that expression? It is a funny way of saying that you are ready to do the thing you want to do, or go to the place you planned, but it's too early yet. You have extra time on your hands. Unfortunately, some Christians think that this life is just something they have to wait through until they get to heaven. They think they are only here killing time. If only they could learn that God has so much more for them right now! Do you remember the answer to this question: "What kind of life did God call Israel to live?" It is: "You shall be holy to me, for I the LORD am holy and have separated you from the peoples, that you should be mine" (Leviticus 20:26). Just as the Israelites were to be holy, God desires all his children now to be busy about being holy. We are to make every effort to be spotless and blameless and to lead lives that are pleasing to Jesus. We don't want to waste any time on this earth. Because of Jesus's return, you should live to please him—you won't be sorry. Your reward will be great indeed!

REFLECTION AND INTERACTION
How should knowing that Jesus will return change what we think, say, and do?

Should we always be thinking of Jesus's return? Why?

All to the Glory of God

Q. Who receives the glory for completing God's promise?

A. To the only God, our Savior, through Jesus Christ our Lord, be glory, majesty, dominion, and authority, before all time and now and forever. Amen. (Jude 25)

Bible Reading: Jude 20–25

Devotional Reading: Praise God! Praise God! He Gets All the Glory for Our Salvation!

These are amazing verses! They show that God alone gets all the glory for our salvation. God is the one who keeps you from falling into sin. God is the one who will bring you into his glorious presence. God is the one who will make you blameless and will fill you with great joy. That means God is the one who should receive all of your praise! The Bible uses the biggest words it can to give praise to God: *glory* and *majesty* and *dominion* and *authority*. Wow! But there is more: not only does God deserve all the praise, he deserves all the praise *all the time*. He deserves it before time began; he deserves it now; and he deserves it forevermore. Praise God! Praise *only* God, through Jesus Christ for our salvation!

REFLECTION AND INTERACTION

Sing the song "Now and Forevermore," written especially for this week and found on page 191.

Can you think of any other ways that we could give praise to God today?

Begin to memorize this week's big picture verse: Jude 25.

> Q. Who receives the glory for completing God's promise?
>
> A. To the only God, our Savior, through Jesus Christ our Lord, be glory, majesty, dominion, and authority, before all time and now and forever. Amen. (Jude 25)

Bible Reading: Romans 11:33–36

Devotional Reading: The Supremacy of God's Glory in Saving a Sinful People

Did you know that there are eight planets in our solar system? What is right in the middle of them? The sun. All eight of the planets revolve around the sun. God is like the sun in this way: all of life revolves around him. God and his glory are right at the very center of the universe. He has planned everything so that people will see how bright, like the sun, his glory is. In fact, our rescue from sin was especially planned to bring him glory! The terrible darkness of our disobedience actually brings God glory. For when God gives us mercy, then his glory and wisdom shine brightly. Do you see how God has designed *everything* to bring him praise? That is why the reading for today said, "For *from* him and *through* him and *to* him are all things." God is at the very center of all things—especially our salvation. "To him be the glory forever!"

REFLECTION AND INTERACTION

What does it mean that God is at the center of the universe?

Try to describe how deep God's wisdom is. What would you compare it to?

> **Q. Who receives the glory for completing God's promise?**
>
> A. To the only God, our Savior, through Jesus Christ our Lord, be glory, majesty, dominion, and authority, before all time and now and forever. Amen. (Jude 25)

Bible Reading: Revelation 19:1–10

Devotional Reading: The Glory of God in Judging Sinners and Giving Mercy to All Who Believe

Imagine the loudest shout that you have ever heard. Now imagine it even louder; imagine millions upon millions of people yelling, "Hallelujah! Salvation and glory and power belong to our God." Our reading today tells us that a day will come when people will give God glory just like that. But do you know why these people are really shouting praises? Two reasons. The first is to give God glory for his judgment. We don't often think of praising God for his judgments, but we will. We will praise God for defeating his enemies. The other reason we will praise God is for his mercy. Those who believe God will receive mercy instead of judgment. They will be invited to God's celebration in heaven with Jesus. What wonderful reasons to shout about God's glory!

REFLECTION AND INTERACTION

Why would God want to be praised for his judgment on sinners?

What does it mean to receive mercy instead of judgment?

Comfort from the King

Q. What will Jesus say when God's promise is complete?

A. Behold, the dwelling place of God is with man. He will dwell with them, and they will be his people, and God himself will be with them as their God. (Revelation 21:3)

Bible Reading: Revelation 21:1–3; 22:1–7, 14; Genesis 2:8–10; 3:23–24

Devotional Reading: A Return to the Tree of Life

Good stories usually finish where they began. The Bible, which is the best story of all, certainly finishes where it began. The Bible began with God creating the heavens and the earth; it began with the terrible disobedience of Adam and Eve; and it began with God's curse upon them. Right at the beginning, God sent Adam and Eve out of the garden of Eden so that they wouldn't eat from the tree of life. Now that we've come to the end of the Bible we are reminded of the beginning. For the Bible ends with a *new* heaven and a *new* earth. It ends with God lifting his curse on us and with his people once again dwelling with him, just like Adam and Eve did in the garden. Yet the end is better than the beginning—because life will be this way forevermore! How amazing! Everyone in the holy city will eat from the tree of life. With our sins traded for Christ's righteousness, we can live forever with God. *We will be his people and he will be our God.*

REFLECTION AND INTERACTION

Why didn't God want Adam and Eve to eat from the tree of life (Genesis 3:22–24)?

Why will he allow people to eat from the tree of life in the new earth?

Memorize this week's big picture verse: Revelation 21:3.

> Q. What will Jesus say when God's promise is complete?
>
> A. Behold, the dwelling place of God is with man. He will dwell with them, and they will be his people, and God himself will be with them as their God. (Revelation 21:3)

Bible Reading: Revelation 22:17–21

Devotional Reading: A Summary of *The Big Picture Family Devotional*

Can you remember when we started this devotional? We learned then that the Bible would be a story about God's kingdom: God's people in God's place under God's rule. It began with God's first people, Adam and Eve, living in God's first place, the garden of Eden. But Adam and Eve rejected God's rule. They had to leave God's place because of their sin. Worse yet, their sin spread; it spread to the whole world. But God had a plan. God chose Abraham and promised to make Abraham into a new people (Israel) and to give him a new place (Canaan). But again, sadly, the new people Israel didn't obey God's rule either. Even though they said, "All that the LORD has spoken we will do" (Exodus 19:8), they kept sinning and turning against God. But God, in spite of their sin, remembered his promise and his plan for a new kingdom people. So he repeated his promise to King David. He promised David that the kingdom people would come from David's offspring. From David would come an eternal kingdom. And that kingdom is the reason why Jesus was born. By paying for our sins on the cross, Jesus made it possible for us to live as his people in his place under his rule. When Jesus returns again, he will take us to that kingdom. That is the wonderful story of God's kingdom! Isn't it great news?

REFLECTION AND INTERACTION

How does it make you feel to know that Jesus is coming soon to take his people to his kingdom?

Thank God for his rescue plan and that Jesus is returning.

Q. What will Jesus say when God's promise is complete?

A. Behold, the dwelling place of God is with man. He will dwell with them, and they will be his people, and God himself will be with them as their God. (Revelation 21:3)

Bible Reading: John 3:16

Devotional Reading: One Final Thought

In olden days, people made garments, things like a sweater or shirt, from a single thread. They wove it and wove it until they had created what they desired. They called such garments *seamless*. They were seamless because no part needed to be stitched to another thread that had been attached in any way. Well, the Bible is a seamless book. It has one thread that has woven a story of the activity of God in human history. And that thread is God's love— God's love for you and me, and for all the families of the earth in Christ. I encourage you to put on the garment of the Bible. Put on the love of God and wear it. Put on Jesus Christ. In Israel's hard and happy history, *Jesus is the big picture*; he is God's forever King.

REFLECTION AND INTERACTION

Have you "put on" Jesus? What does that mean?

Could you retell the big picture of the storyline of the Bible to someone else?

God Completes His Promise

Review 1: Reviewing the Memory Verses

Parental Helps: Memorizing Bible verses is always a good thing to do, but it is especially important when your children are young. Never underestimate their ability to pick these verses up with just a little encouragement from you. The beauty of memorizing the big picture verses we have selected is that they help you and your children trace the storyline of the Bible. Most catechisms have you memorize doctrine in a systematic fashion. The advantage here is that you are learning Bible verses in sequential fashion. However, we want to encourage you to memorize many other parts of the Bible too! You can never have too much of God's Word in your heart.

Review 2: Tracing the Storyline of the Epistles

Parental Helps: The last nine weeks have followed the lines of the gospel.

Spreading the Gospel of Jesus (Question 37)
Defining the Gospel (Questions 38 and 39)
Believing the Gospel (Question 40)
Living the Gospel (Questions 41, 42, and 43)
The Glory of God's Gospel (Question 44)
The Comfort of the Gospel (Question 45)

Spend some time today reinforcing the big picture of these past weeks. You could do this by asking a few simple discussion questions such as:

- Tell me something about how the gospel gets spread to all the families of the earth?
- If someone asked you to explain to them what the gospel is, what might you say? What else would you want to include? How do we receive the gospel?
- Talk to me about what knowing the gospel might mean for how we act and how we treat other people?
- Who is at the center of the gospel? Are you looking forward to the return of Christ? Why?

Review 3: The Importance of Celebrating Accomplishments

Parental Helps: Since you are reading this paragraph, we can assume that you made it to the very end! Wow! That is a great accomplishment, and it ought to be celebrated. Kids need to know that they have completed something. So celebrate! Throw a party for the whole family. Take your child someplace special. Whatever you choose to do, acknowledge the fact that they have worked their way through the entire Bible. They have traced the storyline from Genesis to Revelation. As your mind gets busy with thoughts on how to mark this special occasion, we want to thank you for using this devotional material. It is our prayer that God will use it to train and nurture many people in the Christian faith. May God bless you!

Big Picture Songs

The Creation Song

Genesis 1

Words and Music: Elisabeth Graves

On the first day God made the light, he made the

night, he made the day.__ On the se - cond day God

made the sky,__ oh__ yes, it hap - pened that way.__ On the

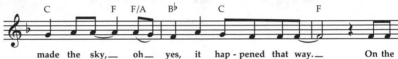

third day God made the seas,__ the dry land and the plants.

__ On the fourth day God made the stars,__ the

It Was Very Good

Genesis 1:31

Music: Gary Rownd

God saw all that he____ had made, all that he____ had made, and it was ve - ry good. It was ve - ry good. It was ve - ry good. It was ve - ry good. It was ve - ry good.____

The Flood Song

Genesis 6:17

Words and Music: Gary Rownd

Ten Commandments

Exodus 20

Music: Gwen Camera

I Will Have Faith in God

Genesis 15:6

Words and Music: Gwen Camera

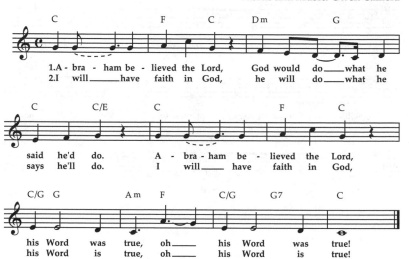

©1999 Gwen Camera

You Are to Be Holy

Leviticus 20:26

Music: Gwen Camera

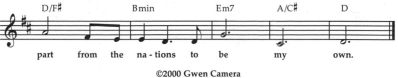

God of the Promise

Deuteronomy 31:7-8; Joshua 1:6; 21:43-45; 23:1-5, 14-16

Words and Music: Tom Fisher

You have kept your prom - is - es, God of the cov - e - nant, God of the prom - ise;

you have kept your prom - is - es, God, you've kept your word.

All of your good prom - is - es, you have kept for you are faith - ful; ___

Fine

In all of your prom - is - es, you've been faith - ful, Lord. 1. The Lord God
2. The Lord God

said, "Be strong and be cou - ra - geous, you must go in - to the
said, "Get read - y now my peo - ple, you will ___ in - to the

land that I have prom - ised." And he said: "No, do not be dis - cour - aged, for the
land that I have prom - ised." So they went, in - to the land he'd giv - en and he

D.C. al Fine

Lord will be with you un - til the ___ end!"
gave them rest ___ on ___ ev - 'ry ___ side! ___

Forever Kingdom

2 Samuel 7:12-13

Text and Music: Douglas O'Donnell

I Am the Resurrection and the Life
John 11:25

Music: Elisabeth Graves

©1999 Elisabeth Graves

I Am the Way
John 14:6

Music: Elisabeth Graves

"My Lord, My God!"
John 20:28

Words and Music: Douglas O'Donnell

©1999 Douglas O'Donnell

No Favorites

Acts 10:42-43

Words and Music: Tom Fisher

Christ is the One whom God the___ Fa - ther has a -
noint - ed___ judge. The___ pro - phets tell the sto - ry___
of his great sal - va - - - tion!
God, we thank you___ that you have no fa - vor - ites;
be - cause of the One you___ sent, we can be your child - dren.
God, we thank you___ that you have no fa - vor - ites;
we will love and trust in you and you will be___ our___ God!

©1999 Tom Fisher

Saved by Grace

Ephesians 2:8-9

Music: Gary Rownd

©1999 Gary Rownd

Now and Forevermore

Jude 25

Music: Gwen Camera

To the on - ly God our Sa - vior,__ be glo - ry, maj - es - ty,__ pow - er and auth - or - i - ty,__ to Je - sus Christ to Je - sus Christ our__ Lord, be-fore all ag - es, now and__ for - e - ver more.

©2000 Gwen Camera

THE BIG PICTURE PICTURE

STORY BIBLE SERIES

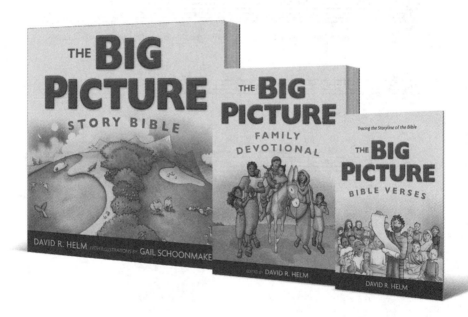

Explore God's Word together as a family with *The Big Picture Story Bible* and see the big picture of God's love for you unfold from Genesis to Revelation. Teach your kids to apply God's Word with *The Big Picture Family Devotional* and help them memorize key Scripture passages with *The Big Picture Bible Verses*.

Download a free audio recording of The Big Picture Story Bible, *read by the author, at* BigPictureStoryBible.com